Dear Ann Volume 1:
Episodes 1-60

Letters to and from Teachers, Students, Parents, and More

By Ann Y. Mouse

Aletheia Pyralis Publishers

For information about special discounts available for bulk purchases, sales promotions, fund-raising and educational needs, please email: devyaschildren@gmail.com

http://www.juliecgilbert.com/

Love Science Fiction or Mystery?

Choose your adventure!

Visit: http://www.juliecgilbert.com/

For details on getting free books.

Dedication:

To the many teachers, parents, friends, colleagues, and random strangers who answered my many questions.

To the future teachers seeking insight or advice.

To the students we serve day in and day out.

Table of Contents:

Chapter 1:
Welcome and Orientation

Disclaimers:

- This was first published on Amazon's Kindle Vella Platform. As the original document is around 600 pages after formatting, I will break it down into multiple volumes. I'll try to find some good stopping points.
- Chapter size may differ greatly as some of the interviews were short and some went on for quite some time. It all depended on the comfort level of the subject.
- All general opinions not attributed to someone else are my own. I know what I know, but I do not know everything. You may disagree with me on some things. That's fine. A difference of opinion is not a threat. To get the most out of this, you'll want to approach the book with an open mind.
- My experience is mainly with suburban United States public schools, though I did a few years in a Christian private school as well.

Introduction:

Dear Reader,

There's a lot of misinformation, hard feelings, hurt feelings, and straight-up very strong opinions about schools. Because children are involved, people often default to defensive mode when problems arise.

Nobody likes the idea that it's their fault something isn't working perfectly, so the blame game begins. It's also very easy to turn school into an us-versus-them thing.

Let's talk.

I'm a strong believer in good communication going a long way to fix issues, but solid communication is a two-way street.

Who am I?

I am a high school Chemistry and Biology teacher with 17+ years of teaching experience.

What you can expect from the series:

- Random opinions provided by me
- Things I do to boost school morale
- Delicate commentary on hot-button topics
- Questions, comments, and concerns raised by parents
- Questions, comments, and concerns raised by former students
- Questions, comments, and concerns raised by former teachers
- Interviews with anybody who will talk with me about education
- Possible profiles of parent types, student types, teacher types, and administrator types

What I want this to be:

Real, honest answers and discussions featuring the problems and concerns facing modern United States schools and their stakeholders.

The recent pandemic has offered some new challenges and opportunities.

Improved technology has also created and solved some problems. I do not envy those who must navigate the emotional landmines inherent to high school. It's been a while since I was a student. Some things the current batch of students face are new this year, let alone the last decade.

That said ...

- Students and their parents (mostly) aren't teachers. They don't understand the pressures that can hit from multiple sides.
- Elementary teachers aren't high school teachers.
- Gym teachers aren't science teachers.

I'll stop there, but the point remains that everybody has a unique perspective. That's what I want to tap into here.

My hope is that the more we learn about the challenges other people are up against, the more empathy we can channel. Problems can't be faced if we don't know they exist.

American culture revolves around dreams of striking it rich through luck or ingenuity, coming from nothing, and working one's way to wealth. On the whole, we're workaholics. It's not entirely healthy, mentally or physically. (I don't need a medical or psychological degree to tell you that. It falls under one of those inconvenient truths everybody ignores.)

On the flipside, *working hard* does not always translate to good grades like we hope it should. (And staring at math homework doesn't magically do that homework. Neither does asking AI to do something for you immediately convey an understanding of the work.)

I've had people tell me that their kid is working on my coursework for about 7 hours a day. (Insert the horror face emoji.)
My response is that nothing we do should take that long and the student should reach out way before knocking his head on it for that long. (Extra help and emailing the teacher are your friends.)

Asking for help is one of the hardest things in the world.
I remember being sick with Covid. It took me almost a full day to work up the courage to ask a friend to grab a thing of milk for me because I was supposed to be quarantining.

Important Note: This is for educational and/or entertainment purposes only. If you find yourself in a dangerous or highly uncomfortable situation, seek proper help from social services or the police. Do not contact me about things that are compulsory reporting situations unless it's well in the past and has been resolved.

Reiterated Disclaimers:
- I will read everything submitted and contact those who request it. However, please understand that I am only a high school teacher.
- I have a master's degree in education but not a doctorate.
- I'm not a lawyer, a psychologist, a lawmaker, a therapist, or a parent.
- What you get in response will be my honest opinion.

Also, note that many things raised won't have an easy answer (or any). I'm gathering stories from as many sides as I can get to talk to me.

If you have a question or story to share, please email **devyaschildren@gmail.com**.

Sincerely,

~Ann

(Yeah, not my real name, but I like my job and want to keep it. When I started this journey a few years ago, I didn't know what to expect. I wanted it to be truly anonymous for a while. The rationale was that I couldn't be completely honest if I had to worry about toeing certain lines for bosses.)

Chapter 2:
Special Guest: Frustrated Former Art Student

Introduction:
Dear Reader,

Today, we get to hear from Frustrated Former Art Student who built a career in the creative arts from the ground up.

Why am I putting this in as the second Chapter?
First, I want the series to be more than just my voice. I only had one experience in elementary, middle, and high school, but there are lessons to be learned from hearing what other people faced along the way.

Second, although the details may differ, I think there's a very real struggle for fine and performing arts to gain a foothold during budget battles, especially when they're up against items that are linked to funding.

~Ann

Note: Any editing I've done has purely been grammatical in nature. These small interviews will feature real people and their experiences.

Tell me about your high school experience.

As a former student, I knew in high school what career I wanted to pursue into adulthood (creative field, cartoonist, illustrator).

The private school I attended only held art classes once a week for 45 minutes (which is pathetic). However, this was, as a teenager, the only world I knew in terms of learning that profession. I looked forward to it each week and took it very seriously.

The biggest concern from this era of my life was that most of the time the biology teacher strong-armed her way into the situation. She would convince the principal that art classes needed to be cancelled each week in order for us to spend extra time on her class doing what she saw as necessary catch-up work.

This created a bad situation during my Junior and Senior years of high school. During the years I was hoping to prepare for either college or a trade school, I was spending the time I should have been pouring into training for the profession I wanted to do doing extra work for a class that one teacher felt was necessary.

As a result of this—and a general lack of resources for creative careers at my school—I was very ill-prepared when graduating and had no idea what to do in terms of looking for a creative career. The school treated this as though it was a non-career and did not merit the time or resources for me.

One teacher in particular was very controlling and wrecked a lot of opportunities. One of my biggest teenage regrets was the lack of help from my school and its staff and the general dismissive attitude for the career I had chosen.

I wasted many years after high school doing college work for a degree I didn't want and pursuing obvious dead-end leads for creative work. These could have been avoided if I had had proper instruction as a teenager.

This experience has always given me a mental picture of other students—kids—who could be in a similar situation. I have met individuals like this in my adult years, people who have dealt with dismissive attitudes about creative careers or goals by parents or school faculty. I have seen the resulting damage done.

Many times, students go off to a very expensive art school unprepared, get into massive debt and are not ready for the professional world. In other instances, they quit their creative goals and fall into some other more accepted profession due to pressure from their family or friends. I cannot help but think school faculty and parents could do better to support these kinds of kids, who have a legitimate career goal and dreams for the future.

My response:
Thank you for sharing your experience. I'm glad things worked out for you eventually, and I agree that there are likely students who would benefit greatly from increased school support for the arts. Even the small step of being taken seriously can go a long way in building confidence in one's work.

Takeaways:
- The arts don't often get the support they deserve, and there are legitimate careers in the field.
- There are different kinds of kids. (I've seen struggling science students who can memorize whole plays or show me eight sketchbooks of amazing drawings.)
- Dismissive attitudes have real-world consequences.

Chapter 3:
Why are All the Teachers Complaining?

Introduction:

Dear Reader,

All is such a strong word, and there are always multiple sides to a story.

Complaints make better stories.

Venting in safe spaces is healthier than bottling stuff. Unfortunately, social media tends to make even that far more public than it should.

What teachers (usually) love about teaching...

- The kids.
- Their subject.
- The pride of school community.
- Sharing their passion for all of the above.

Teaching isn't only about conveying the pertinent points of a subject to the next generation of students.

What teachers expected to have to do when they signed up for the career ...

- Teach a subject or a skill.
- Submit lesson plans early.
- Grade assessments and other work in a timely fashion.
- Spend their days with elementary, middle school, or high school students.

What teachers are expected to do in addition to the above ...

- (Sometimes) buy their own supplies.
- Entertain kids.
- Catch failing kids.
- Abide by 504 and Individualized Education Plans (IEPs), which can have anything and everything from legitimate give this kid extra time on assessments concerns to super vague provide preferential seating to oddities like let the kid go for a walk at any time.
- Foster a positive, safe learning environment.
- (Sometimes, especially in the lower grades) Decorate the classroom.
- Create and implement hands-on activities.
- Deal with kids wherever they're at.
- Prepare students to be good digital citizens.
- Teach students to make better moral decisions like don't cheat even if you can get away with it.
- Formally and informally assess student progress in your classroom.
- Get students to pass state tests. (Teachers often get slammed for teaching to the test, but they're also evaluated by how many kids pass said test.)
- Monitor behaviors.

- Deal with this random phenomenon of at least 2 kids needing to sharpen a pencil the exact second you want to say something instructional.
- Keep a cover-your-butt log of interventions tried on a student.
- Modify workloads for certain students. (There are some legitimate reasons to do this, but that has more to do with acute life events, not the kid just can't do the current work.)
- (Occasionally) Deal with a rotating lunch period or no time to eat.
- Cover classes for colleagues who are absent because there is a shortage of substitutes. (Note: In this case, teachers do get paid something, but some people would rather have the period off to eat, gather brain cells, use the restroom, or all of these.)
- Fill in paperwork for struggling students.
- Filling in paperwork to go on field trips.
- Having field trips canceled.
- Dealing with seizures in the classroom. (It's happened at least twice over the course of my career thus far.)
- Telling a student to get off a counter.
- Deal with large class sizes.
- Support and challenge the highfliers.
- Keep certain kids away from each other.
- Deal with student addiction to phones.
- Attend professional development.
- Measure student progress in multiple ways, including long-term endeavors.
- (Sometimes) Integrate the latest and greatest technology.
- Keep kids from doing drugs.
- Defend lessons to parents. (This one should pretty much never happen.)

- Plan bathroom breaks very carefully.
- Teach kids basic things like we don't hit each other and we don't eat gum that was stuck to the underside of a desk.
- Deal with disrespect from students and parents.
- Provide a supportive ear for students when necessary.
- Assure, reassure, and re-reassure parents, guidance, and administration that you're doing everything possible to see that every student shows progress, even the lazy ones.

Why are teachers feeling overwhelmed?

A lot of the job is non-stop problem solving. That takes mental energy. Some people think deeper on things than others, so the energy toll is even higher.

Teachers also have their own lives. This includes personal obligations, families to care for, and trying to project the illusion of keeping it together even if they're struggling.

Please don't take this list as pure excuses. I am trying to show you some of what goes on behind the scenes, so you have a better understanding of where some of the strain is coming from.

~Ann

Chapter 4:
Special Guest: Frustrated Former English Teacher

Introduction:
Dear Reader,

We recently got to hear from a Frustrated Former Student. It's a good time for balance.

Let's hear some concerns raised by a former public school teacher.

~Ann

Tell us your story.
I wrote an entire book dealing with the issues of attending and teaching in a public high school. (It was my therapy after being harassed by students out of the classroom after teaching for 15 years.) I had the highest test scores by my sophomore students on their state tests that year and even got remedial senior English students to pass their exit exams and get out the door.

Where did all the bad blood come from for the cohort that had me diving for the exit for self-preservation?
I blame the standards-based grading movement along with the idea

that nearly all students have so many deep-seated issues they cannot be held accountable for learning or treating each other civilly or treating their teachers with respect.

Side note (a.k.a. me rudely butting in to emphasize a point): This is really well put. There are certainly situations where kids can and should get modified workloads, but if students are never forced to earn their grades, it leads to a dangerous sense of entitlement. More on that later.

What's at the heart of the problem?
Students and parents want to see A's on those report cards, but don't want to put in the effort of learning what is required to earn those A's. Then add in *restorative justice* where the victims sit across the table from their tormentors. It's no wonder students don't want to come to school, and the bullies feel they can continue to bully without consequences.

I loved teaching (in a public school) and loved the students who tried hard to learn.

What do you do now and what do you love about it?
I do military counseling. I love the mutual respect of counseling those on a military base to get started or continue their college educations.

I see the impact on those who have not learned basic skills during their K-12 education. Lack of basic skills holds Service Members back from their chosen MOS (military operational specialty). Many times, foreign nationals, who also serve our nation, meet the scores needed for those choices over and above many Americans.

What do you think the problem is?
Reassessment and lack of deadlines lead to procrastination. Lack of accountability for uncivil behavior only empowers those to create more chaos.

I was a well-respected teacher for 15 years and then ran into a cohort of students with their parents who didn't want to learn or to <u>earn</u> grades, but felt entitled to bully me and others.

It took time for me to find the next place I can serve and make a difference in lives, where I am respected. Now, I have the upmost respect for those I serve and a safe environment for all of us to thrive.

My response:
I'm so glad you found the right place for you. Respect is a word often thrown around that few truly grasp, but it's so powerful.
In a way, your story echoes that of the Frustrated Former Student. It sounds like schools and a small subset of parents failed to provide the environment needed to do your job to the best of your abilities.

The Service Members are lucky to have you helping them along their career journeys. Thanks for taking the time to share your experience with us.

Takeaways:
- Accountability is important.
- Support should not mean you get something for nothing.
- Bullying isn't confined to the school setting. Adults (parents, administrators, and teachers) are not immune to the tendency to act like tyrants when they don't get their way. The semi-unfortunate thing is that bullies (squeaky wheels) tend to get their way because giving in is the easiest option, even if it is ultimately detrimental to the student.

Chapter 5:
Teacher Responsibility for Student Grades Only Goes So Far

Introduction:

Dear Reader,

Aside: I'm hoping to eventually get some parents and more former students to share their experiences and stories, but since my sphere of influence is heavily weighted to other teachers, these entries are going to initially contain a lot of teacher-specific problems and concerns.

I received the following message from someone called Frustrated Teacher. I assure you this is a different person than the Frustrated Former English Teacher we heard from before.

The situation:

Dear Ann,

I taught public school 20 years ago, before I realized that it wasn't where I needed to be.

I taught beginning computer literacy, which included keyboarding.

One day, I had a conference with an angry parent because her straight-A daughter had a B in my class because she (the student) was struggling with typing without looking at her hands!

There was no tutoring or extra credit I could give the child, she just needed to practice, but that wasn't what the parent wanted to hear. To her (the parent), I was *ruining* the child's GPA.

~Frustrated Teacher

My response:

That's a tough situation to be in. I don't know what pressures you got from the administration on this matter, but that could make all the difference.

Emphasis: Support from administration can go a long way in making or breaking a teacher who finds themselves in a similar situation.

Although I have never taught computers or typing, I am somewhat familiar with the topic raised from both sides (as a student and as a teacher).

When I was in high school, my GPA was held down by gym class because the teacher didn't feel that anybody was perfect in the first quarter. I didn't necessarily agree with the decision, but it was the teacher's to make. I'm no worse for wear because of it.

On the flip side, I'm very familiar with the attitudes students and parents have concerning grades.

When students do well, it's easy for them to claim credit. When they don't do well, suddenly it's the teacher's fault for one reason or another.

Long story short:

Grades are earned by students.

Longer version with more details, including the key difference:

Teachers are not responsible for the grades students earn. Teachers are responsible for setting up the criteria that defines how a grade is earned.

In the situation Frustrated Teacher landed in, the criteria for an A involved typing without looking at the keys. Outsider looking in, that seems a reasonable expectation for a typing class.

Some skills hinge on practice.

With what I teach, some students can look at one example and immediately pick up on the concept. Others need to see a dozen examples to even begin comprehending what's happening.

Flipside:

There are times when the criterion for earning an A seems to be shifting sand. Sometimes, there are reasons for such shifts, and sometimes, it's completely random.

I had a parent unofficially ask what to do when you and the teacher find yourself at an impasse concerning your child. (I don't know enough of the situation yet to turn it into its own Chapter, so I'll mention it here.)

That too is a tough situation. I'd suggest stepping back and evaluating from three perspectives.

- One, what is the source of the conflict? Is there an answer to resolve this conflict?
- Two, how uncomfortable is the situation? Is it mildly uncomfortable or dangerously uncomfortable or something in between? To that end, can your child stick it out or would a switch in class be the better road to take?
- Three, what are the long-term consequences of leaving the situation as is or pushing for some sort of change?

There's no easy, pat answer that works all the time. Based on the answers for these questions, use your best judgment in devising a plan to address the underlying issues with the teacher, the administration, your child, or some combination thereof.

Note: Many people skip right to attack mode. That's never a great starting point.

Takeaways:
- Teachers set up criteria for which performance earns which grade.
- Students earn their grades.
- Some skills can be modeled but mastery can directly correlate to practice.

Chapter 6:
Special Guest: Concerned Educator's Journey

Introduction:

Dear Reader,

Although the focus is on K-12 education, there are many other institutions that need skilled, dedicated people to take up the title of teacher.

Our special guest today has held several different jobs. This is normal. Some people spend their whole careers in one place, and others only spend seasons in a place before moving on.

Burnout is a possibility. Knowing when to move on is important for one's own sanity.

~Ann

Hi. Welcome. Tell us about yourself and your journey.

When I first started as a high school ELA (English Language Arts) teacher, I didn't fully understand how much was involved in getting everything done for class and beyond it, including the planning, meetings, paperwork, cleaning, and buying much of my own supplies.

While many can get through it, even lately with the pandemic, the stress and overwhelming demands affected my mental health.

I wanted to do my best because that has been what I've always done, but also because of my students.

Even though I couldn't handle staying in the job after several months, I still think about those students to this day.

Thanks for sharing. What would you tell your past self?

I would like to tell my past self that your heartbreak and darkness after making the biggest decision that you'll ever make to date at that time would be worth it.

What are you up to today?

I ultimately found my place in Adult Education. It's a part-time job, but it led me to realize that I could be an ESL instructor. Eventually I got a chance to move up to academic adviser and test proctor in my Adult Education program. Now, I have the space to do that work, along with my additional passions: writing and web content management.

When I was a high school teacher, I didn't have time for my writing. Now, I'm a published author. I want to let new teachers realize there is another path available to you. If you struggle, reflect and find an option that works better for you.

Now, I work towards also making sure that I fight for changes in education so it's better for new teachers. There're so many stressors, and now, people don't even respect teachers.

Even politicians who want to direct what teachers do in the classroom or books that students can read. I'm concerned about that. We're also all struggling still with the pandemic. We have to find ways to make sure that we can make changes to benefit our students, but also educators, staff, and everyone involved with education.

Concerned Educator's question for me:
What do you think would be ways we can make changes?

My response:
I'll answer the last question first. Changes likely need to be made in multiple places. Improving communication—one aim for this series—is a start, but there's unfortunately not a one-size fits all solution. What works in urban schools may not work in rural schools or suburban schools. Same for public vs. private schools. This topic will likely become its own essay later because there's a lot to unpack, but in short, here are some helpful steps:

- Acknowledge there's a problem
- Improve communications
- Fix what we can, where we can
- Current educators may need to enter other arenas and take up the fight as lawmakers and advocates

Mental health is a major concern. It has become a buzzword, but nobody (so far) has had satisfactory answers to adequate relief. Schools like to throw around phrases like self-care, but if it's not backed up by any kind of change, the mental stressors are going to remain in play, and people are going to continue leaving the profession in droves.

Takeaways:
- Schools need dedicated teachers.
- People need their mental health.
- They're not mutually exclusive, but when the two points come to blows, side with your mental health. (Staying in a toxic place is not worth it, even if there are some wonderful kids you'll miss dearly.)

Chapter 7:
What Do We Do About
Dumbing Down and Over-Testing?

Introduction:

Dear Ann,

When I started teaching seniors 8 years ago, we taught British literature sequentially. Each era featured lessons on the time period, vocabulary, and great classics such as *Beowulf, Canterbury Tales, Macbeth, Frankenstein,* and *Pride and Prejudice.* They were challenging, but kids learned continuity and how to navigate hard things.

Teachers are now mandated by the district to give several diagnostic reading tests (not to mention being displaced from rooms and WiFi to accommodate tests, retests, and practice tests by the state for underclassmen), and they are forced into "performance assessments" for our students. That doesn't leave time for anything but short pieces with short activities for kids with short attention spans. If and when kids fail to turn in those assignments, and many do, credit recovery is there for them to earn the "P" for passing in just 4 short afternoons ... if they will just show up.

All this dumbing down is happening simultaneously to the propagandizing of students that they ALL need to go to college. It is both ironic and cruel unless colleges are dumbing down as well (a truly frightening thought).

What are some solutions for individual teachers to combat the dumbing down of our schools?

Sincerely,

Teacher Feeling Helpless
(A.k.a. Veteran Teacher and Former Student)

My response:
You raised a lot of great points.

You're not alone. Practically every subject area is getting hit with things like this. We're asked to make and give special assessments at the beginning, middle, and end of the year to measure student progress.

I'm sure the terminology will differ from place to place, and it changes a lot. I won't tell you what my state calls them this year because it's likely to be something else by next year. They're kind of ridiculous though because it boils down to ... in the beginning the students get everything wrong because we haven't covered any material yet. At the mid-point they know some stuff but not a lot because we haven't learned it yet. At the end of the year, the hope is that the kids master it, but the truth is that often they still get a lot of stuff wrong because they're used to cramming and dumping information for individual tests. (And they're busy taking standardized tests for every other subject matter.)

All that to say, the problem is real and pervasive.

The greatest change would probably happen at levels well above our paygrade. That said, I'm reminded of the fact that even the largest trees in the forest start as tiny seeds.

Also, you asked for suggestions individual teachers could implement. You may have already thought of this, but perhaps don't try to regain the entire hill we lost due to dumbing down. Instead creep forward a few yards.

By this, I mean pick one of those classics a marking period and cover it in depth. You'll still get interrupted, but fit longer term items in the space you would have stuck short things. Yes, kids have short attention spans. But turn it around on them.

Really, really random suggestions:

- You could try making it a project. Have students do a video, poster project, live skit, comic book, traditional report, or whatever medium you like. It could even be a student choice.
- Provide some low-hanging fruit for the slackers but be clear that it doesn't get full credit.
- Challenge students to find 7 differences between a movie version and the book or play.
- Assign the stories to different groups for a project. Have the kids make a group homework sheet with a key.
- **Warning:** you must check it because their work can be shoddy.
- Try flat-out bribery. You'd be surprised what kids do for scratch-and-sniff stickers and Dum Dums.
- Try to instill in them that getting by may serve them today, but they should always expect better from themselves. Explore their interests. They typically will pour large parts of their time, energy, and effort into something.
- How much freedom do you have with picking books? You could ask for donations from indie authors until you get 25-50 books (or whatever a class set is), then have the students pick one and look for whatever vocab word or grammar thing you're looking for that day or week.

- Make it a coffee club. (Get permission to implement this one.) You could probably even ask the kids for supplies. Kids read a book of their own choice (with some criteria) and then discuss (argue) stuff you want them to look for in books. No report, no coffee. Let natural selection happen.

Takeaways:
- I guess the short answer is that if you want to fight this battle on an individual basis, you're going to have to get creative.
- Redefine what is doable and what constitutes acceptable losses in this battle.

Maybe a comprehensive appreciation for British literature is out of reach, but perhaps a love of books and the English language is still attainable.

Chapter 8:
Special Guest: Frustrated Elementary Teacher with Multiple Concerns

Introduction:
Note: I'll respond in between sections because the letter raises a few different concerns.

Issue 1:
Dear Ann,

My frustration stems from the fact that not all children are able to get the services they need due to lack of budget, lack of parental support at home, lack of Title 1 funding, and so forth.

We are not allowed to retain children who may simply need more time to mature emotionally or academically, because God forbid their self-esteem will be crippled in kindergarten.

My response to not holding kids back.
Personally, I ended up a year behind the other kids in elementary. It went fine for me. I think this policy is more about the bruising of parent egos than it is about the kids. And you are right, their

self-esteem would be fine.

Issue 2:

Half of the students at my school are reading below grade level and the administration can only blame the teachers. They won't even think about changing the curriculum. Instead, we are told to differentiate for those students by using a different curriculum, a curriculum which, by the way, general education teachers have received no training on. We are expected to simply just research it or consult with someone who has received the training. (Or worse, pay out of pocket for training.)

My response to curriculum concerns:

Can you make up your own curriculum or get something from Teachers Pay Teachers or friends at a different school? People have been doing this a lot longer than you and I have. I'm not saying that everything is transferrable, especially if it's a lot older, but it doesn't hurt to ask.

That's a lot of extra work for you, which isn't entirely fair and that stinks. People (districts included) will always try to get what they can from you for as little as possible. I guess the best you can do is clearly define how far you're willing to retreat before making a stand. Once you get tenure, you do have a bit more pushback power.

Issue 3:

Another concern is that there is no discipline for students. We are expected to constantly reward children for being decent, kind humans but ignore the bad things they do like hit, bite, spit, etc. Administration is lowering the bar each year for discipline. I'm not even allowed to keep children inside from recess or give them lunch detention.

My response to the lowered discipline bar.

Ideally, the foundation of discipline should be in the home, but I can see how it would be frustrating for you to have no recourse besides "please, stop doing that because it's not nice." Maybe try extra rewards for decency. (Rewards are a privilege and privileges can be taken away.)

There may not be an easy answer to this one.

Issue 4:

Finally, the line for parents to drop off students in the morning is about 5 miles long and causing major traffic jams all over town. The teachers are being told to arrive a half-hour early in order to get a parking space. It's hard to drive around traffic when there is only one entrance into the parking lot. This is non-contractual time.

We should have our own separate entrance. Instead, the principal claims that the town owns the land where the teachers want to build a new parking lot and he claims that the district cannot get permission from the town. Seems odd to me because the drop-off line traffic is affecting the town too. I hope the town would want to collaborate with the district to make it work. (Or I'm being terribly naïve. I'm probably being terribly naïve.)

Anyway, one day, a parent hit a teacher I work with in the parking lot. So now, not only are we being told to arrive early. Our safety is also in jeopardy. My car was even hit one day by a parent. Thankfully, no damage just scratches.

These are just a few examples of the egregious things happening in my school district.

My response:

The traffic situation is unique to every school. I always arrive early because I like doing so. It's peaceful. Maybe have teachers who live in the town spearhead a movement to get a separate parking lot. Most towns have meetings where people can raise concerns. Crazy traffic seems like a worthy problem for the town to tackle. (I'm assuming this is a public school.)

If things get too bad, try looking for work elsewhere, but understand that every school has some issues. They may not be to this degree or even these exact problems, but it will be something.

One more question for me:
Do you think these concerns would still exist at a private Christian school?

My response:
Having worked in both settings, I'll say that these concerns may not exist in a private Christian school, but they could. It's likely you'd get a different set of concerns. You'd likely still get pushback over the idea of holding a student back. You'd probably get more support on discipline, a lot more freedom with curriculum, and probably wouldn't have a parking problem.

On the other hand, you're also likely to take a steep cut in pay compared to a public school.

Takeaways:
- Some people find their forever school right away and others bounce around.
- There will always be kids who need the light you can bring into their lives.

Chapter 9:
How to Handle the (Apparent)
Apathetic Parent

Introduction:

Dear Reader,

Today's question is a short one but a doozy.

~Ann

Dear Ann,

How do you address a parent who seems not to be concerned with their child's lack of progress in school?

~Frustrated Teacher

My response:

I'm tempted to say don't do a darn thing because as long as they don't care, they won't bother you. However, it doesn't quite work like that. Often, teachers (unfairly) get held responsible for a child's lack of progress.

Administration and guidance will tell you to contact the parents. Sometimes, you get a response, and sometimes you don't. In a way, apathy is better than irrational blame from that quarter.

To your specific question, I'd recommend being as clear and polite as possible. Include all the pertinent details like what the child is missing and what can be done at this point. It's better if the child can still earn some credit for late assignments. Straight notifications of failure with no recourse is a much more awkward conversation.

Send multiple notifications if you must.

Ideally, the parents will work with you to help motivate a child to succeed. That said, this isn't the case for many kids for various reasons.

If parent participation isn't going to be a thing, then keeping them informed is the next best thing.

Side note: If there's a language barrier, I'd recommend using Google translate and then having somebody proofread the email. Even if there isn't a language barrier, getting a second set of eyes on an email you intend to send may be helpful.

Communicate in a method that's comfortable for you. Some people prefer phones. I prefer emails. It gives me the chance to check my wording carefully. There's also a record of the notification.

Student struggles and the causes thereof could fill multiple pages.

Important points to convey in your message (be that phone or email):
- The basic situation – I'm guessing this has to do with the student failing or almost failing or missing a lot of assignments.

- What needs to happen (and by when!) – If there is a lot of missing work, try to prioritize by what will give the student the most credit for the least amount of effort. (I know a lot of you just cringed. Sorry, but I promised to be honest. If a student is borderline failing you, they're likely also flubbing school elsewhere, getting some of your makeup work could take a miracle. Remember a passing student is one less reason for admin to breathe down your neck.)
- What has been tried – Reminded student of missing work, set up an appointment for extra help, etc.
- (If possible) something you appreciate about the student – if you legitimately can't think of any redeeming qualities, then end with a pleasantry or a hope. (I.e., Thank you for your time. I hope we can work together to see your child succeed.)

Do parents truly not care?
Every situation is unique. I'd venture to say many cases where the parent doesn't seem to care, they're overwhelmed and out of their league when it comes to the problems their child faces and makes by actions or inactions.

They might be too busy with the stress from their job or sick folks or a lingering disease. They may also just be tired of fighting their kid on multiple points. Whatever the underlying reason, do your best to clearly communicate the situation.

Another approach:
You may have better luck reaching the child from your side than going through the parent. Keep the parent and guidance in the loop, but also, notify the child of your concerns.

If they're in middle school or high school, it's time they learned to solve some of their own problems.

If they're in elementary school, try some direct approaches, then keep a log of the strategies you try. What does the kid need? Some need to be involved. Some need to be left alone. The way one kid functions will likely not be the way another does.

Here's one of those uncomfortable but necessary reality checks.

Teachers have a finite amount of time and energy. Clearly communicate the situation. Do everything in your power to overcome whatever is preventing the kid from succeeding. Then, move on with a clear conscience.

I've had students fail my class, but I also make it such that one must actively try to fail.

Takeaways:

- You can't control the parent's reaction.
- Be as clear in your communication as possible.
- Offer a gameplan for the student to follow to succeed.
- Don't feel guilty if every effort still fails to get the student to do what's necessary to earn success. Failure's not comfortable, but it can be a wakeup call for some.

Chapter 10:
Special Guest: Concerned Teacher – Let's Talk HIB from a Different Perspective

Note: HIB stands for Harassment, Intimidation, and Bullying.

Observation: The word bullying has been misused and overused to the point that people are just downright confused as to what that entails.

Introduction:
Background:
We talk a lot about what the kids should do if someone is harassing, intimidating, or bullying them. They should tell a teacher, go to guidance, or tell another trusted adult. This kicks off a whole chain of events wherein the matter legally needs to be settled quickly.

But ... what happens if a student is harassing a teacher?

The sad truth is that teachers don't have much recourse when it comes to uncomfortable situations started by students.

Dear Ann,

I have some stories to share with you.

Story 1: (probably all too common)
An electives teacher is leaving my school because the administration isn't handling things well. Part of the reason she's checking out is she overheard a kid say she's hot.

My response to story 1:
What created the perfect storm in the first place? Kids are being dumped into electives to tick a box when they have zero interest in that subject.

As any of the lovely training videos we have to watch annually would tell you. If something said, even in gest, makes a person feel uncomfortable, it's considered harassment and highly frowned upon.

Story 2: (even creepier)
The atmosphere in the classroom is uncomfortable. There's a lot of weird subtext going around. In high school (especially the upper grades), you get boys in men's bodies. What they think is appropriate to say is appalling and they're not being held accountable for it.

Recently, a young man in my classroom began saying odd things like we (he and I) should get matching tattoos. (He then wrote my name on his arm with a marker.) I didn't think much of it at the time.

Later, the young man asked if I was related to someone with the same last name. Caught off guard, I confirmed that I was but didn't say how I was related to him. (The name brought up was my husband's name.)

Fast forward 3-4 days, my husband's cell phone got a crank call wherein the young man told him (my husband) that I was having an affair with another teacher. Luckily, I was standing right there, and my husband knows the other teacher mentioned.

More calls came in.

The kid tried to disguise his voice in some of them, but his identity was pretty obvious. Incidentally, he also had a cackling sidekick with him while he made the calls.

Needless to say, this freaked my husband (and me) out. He didn't want me walking the dog that night because anybody who could find our phone number could also find our home address.

I emailed the administration, and we had a conference with the young man and his father.

Thankfully, the child's father seemed shocked by his behavior, but overall, nothing happened. The kid's back to his overconfident, cocky little self.

What did I get? An apology from the administration. Just what I always wanted.

So, my question is this: what should teachers do when they're being harassed by a student?

~Concerned Teacher

My response to story 2:
Wow. That sounds like something I'd make up in a fiction story and then get slammed for in reviews because it's not realistic.

First, I'm sorry you have to deal with this. (This isn't me accepting any sort of blame for the events that transpired. I'm acknowledging that it's a terrible spot for anybody to be in and making a general apology on behalf of humanity.)

Second, I'm sure you document everything, but just in case you didn't think to do so because incidents leading up to that were so small, go back and document everything you can remember, including dates and times if necessary.

Fairy-tale, best-case scenario: The kid had his laugh, got his scolding, and learned not to cross that line again. I hope this not only for your sake but also for the kid's sake. It's a very disturbing pattern of behavior. If he doesn't get the message now, while he's young, he's in for a world of complications when he grows out from under the legal protections of being a minor.

Unfortunately, discipline lies almost completely in the hands of the parents when it comes to a minor. In extreme cases, you could hit the child with a restraining order, but that's about it. While good in theory, I have my doubts about those being helpful because anybody willing to cause a situation that prompts a restraining order already has very little respect for other people or the law.

Takeaways: (for anyone in similar difficult situations)

- To the best of your abilities, protect yourself both mentally and physically. (Resigning shouldn't be a first option, but it's there. Your health and safety trumps most other considerations.)
- The kid is 100% in the wrong. Hopefully, a sit-down chat is enough to press home the seriousness of the offense.
- If similar behavior continues, seek legal counsel and/or seek to get the child removed from your classroom. Schools are all about mental health this and that. Hold them to it on this point. (If they give you any lines about it being difficult to accomplish, you let them know what a smoking load of smelly horse crap that is. They bend over backwards for the kids—switching schedules to honor whims. They can fix it so you don't have to deal with this kid for the year.)

Chapter 11:
General Opinion: Thoughts on Lack of Respect

Introduction:

Dear Reader,

What can be done about the lack of respect afforded to teachers? Nobody's point-blank raised the question with me, but I've heard enough grumblings and read enough social media posts and articles to know it's a concern weighing heavily upon many teachers.

It's often cited by those leaving the profession.

~ Ann

My response:

As always, there's a short answer and a longer answer.

Short answer: We can try to educate the public.

Longer answer:

For simplicity, I'm going to limit the scope of stakeholders to 4:

students, teachers, parents, and administrators. In an ideal world, respect would go every direction.

Side note: There are many more people who have a vested interest in keeping a school community running. There are also many more people employed by schools than teachers and administrators.

Working theory (because that sounds so much cooler than random guess) of what caused the problem:

The best solutions spring from an understanding of the heart of the problem. I think the foundation of this problem rests in three things: apathy, ignorance, and stress.

Apathy: Apathy gets a bad reputation, but in a way, it's a defense mechanism. On the whole, if something's not directly affecting us, we're wired not to care.

Side note: There are people with great empathy for others. More often than not, that just means their mental health suffers whenever they have a hard time shutting off the influx of bad news.

Ignorance: The truest way to understand something is to experience it. In other words, non-teachers don't know much about the profession.

Bunny trail: There may be a few books featuring teachers as the main characters, but it's not quite to the level of cops, firefighters, EMTs, doctors, or lawyers. The lack of coverage may contribute to widespread misunderstandings about what teachers do. To be fair, situations very widely within schools, let alone across different levels and types of schools.

Stress: The pandemic cast a light on the teaching profession because everything changed in the span of a week. Stress comes from many quarters, but it's human nature to become wrapped up in personal problems, which gives one less time, patience, and energy for what others face.

Do we understand respect?

According to Google, there are two definitions of respect. One has to do with admiration for some great quality or accomplishment. The other has to do with regarding the wishes, rights, and traditions of others.

I think there may be a disconnect between the types of respect. Everybody—teachers included—likes when they get the first type and expects the second type. But teaching situations differ so much that people don't think to afford the second brand of respect.

Devil's advocate: It can be difficult to respect rights that are only implied and not reality.

Teachers have and always will attempt to instill basic human lessons like spitting at your classmates isn't nice. However, a lot of that training, which forms the basic of a kid's notions about respect, come from home. When the home breaks down, this becomes harder.

Teachers have a public relations problem.

There's a perception that anybody can become a teacher. This leads to the assumption that it's an easy job and by extension less worthy of respect (admiration).

Teaching is not a cool job like joining the Drug Enforcement Agency, the Federal Bureau of Investigation, or saving lives through surgery. It's a necessary, but not always glamorous job that requires a lot of basic problem-solving skills.

Why don't teachers feel respected?

There are shifting sands of dos and don'ts. What's okay one year isn't in a different year.

They are held responsible for the actions or inactions of others. If a student is failing, the first thing most administrators and some parents think isn't what the heck is this kid doing or not doing? It's usually, what is the teacher doing about it?

If a class is out of control, it's often the teacher who gets a hard look for lack of classroom management skills.

What exactly are teachers looking for?

Backup. Support. Protection. A way out of the blame-game. The irony is that one of the key responsibilities of teaching in a classroom setting is providing a safe, supportive environment for learning to take place in.

Not every parent is a yeller, but the loud ones are the memorable ones. Unfortunately, there's no way around the mentality of the squeaky wheel gets oil. But if everybody caves to demands like change my kids grade because s/he worked really hard, we're in trouble in the long run.

What can be done? (These are also takeaways.)

- Wherever possible educate the public about what teachers really do. (It's way more than teach a curriculum.)
- Be proactive with communication, both good and bad concerning all students.
- When necessary, educate the students on what respect is and is not. Modeling can be a powerful tool.
- Respect should go every direction. Teachers only have control over a few of these (directly themselves, indirectly students and parents and administrators). Even when people do dumb things, try to find something about them you can respect.

Chapter 12:
Special Guest: Curious Teacher – Can Classroom Management be Taught? Part 1

Introduction:

Dear Ann,

Can classroom management be taught in a real classroom setting?
~Curious Teacher

My response:

Yes and no, for many reasons, though more no than yes. Bear with me now that I've thoroughly confused you.

Classroom management techniques that might work if the stars align right can be taught in grad school, professional development, and such. However, most veteran teachers will tell you that every class is different.

A colleague of mine once said that managing a class is like raising a kid. What works for one will not work for another. (To one kid, sitting in a corner for a set amount of time could be a horrible, no good, awful punishment to be avoided at all costs. Another kid will happily perch wherever, retreat into their mind, and have a lovely time communing with the random paint chips in the corner.)

Note: Some of the techniques are specific to certain ages.

Possible classroom management techniques: (mostly aimed at middle or high school because that's my wheelhouse)

Get to know the students.
To me, this one gets top priority. I ask students random questions on a regular basis. This gives me great insight into their lives. It's limited to what they want to tell me, but I love learning these little tidbits. Every little thing you can do to let them know they're important and unique can help.

Communicate regularly with all student homes.
I don't like using the phone, but I email all parents regularly (one mass email per class) to keep them up to date with what we're doing and ask for their help with encouraging the kids to keep on top of their workloads. This works for me. It may or may not work for you. If you hate email with a passion, it may not be the best technique for you.

Create classroom norms.
I've seen a lot of support for people inviting student input and guiding them toward certain norms that you want anyway. This is mostly for elementary classrooms. In high school, basically, just be clear about what you expect of the students and what they can and can't do.

Use positive reinforcement.
Praise and niceties can go a long way in keeping the classroom atmosphere on the warm fuzzy side of the spectrum.

Engage in tangible positive reinforcement.
Okay, I mean stickers, eraser caps, shiny pencils, and Dum Dums (or some other allergy-free candy). Never underestimate the power

of the sticker. Also, you can get great deals on stickers.

Find a gimmick that works with your personality.
If you love video games, fill your classroom with video game stuff. Many kids will relate to it.

Engage the students in stuff they like.
Once again, choose stuff that you like as well. If you're not genuine about something, they'll pick up on it immediately.

Use phone privileges (and phone jail) to your advantage.
This will vary per school because districts choose to handle this issue differently. If you're allowed to choose, make clear that letting them keep the phones is a privilege that can and will go away if abused.

Choose battles and class privileges well.
Kids love sitting on counters. If it won't drive you completely batty and you have counters, let them sit on it while working. Let them listen to music if they're doing independent work. These are just samples of privileges that can be extended to the class. I always let them know that I have a set amount of stuff for them to do. If they can get that done before the class time is over, they can have the extra time to relax, get work done for other classes, nap, or play on their phones. They 100% choose the phone, but it sounds better that there are many options.

Turn the disruptive students into helpers.
If there are multiple disruptive students, this can be difficult. I've had some success with having the Class Wanderer write the answers on the board. It kept him engaged and on task, and I think he enjoyed it.

Directly address inappropriate behaviors like calling out randomness.
This one may not be doable in lower levels, especially middle school where everything is a personal crisis. If you have the right relationship with high school students, you can usually tell them to their faces when they're being difficult.

Offer grace where you can.
Teachers have the ability to accept late work, give second chances, extend extra credit, assignment redos or corrections, and so forth. You don't want to overdo this one or deadlines won't have any meaning. After a deadline passes, have some mark that is the new max score. (There should be a late penalty.)

Use teacher voice sparingly but to good effect
Most teachers have developed this scary bellow where if used the kids know for sure they've screwed up big time. Other teachers can also use deadly-calm voice with much the same results. You do not want to regularly scare the bejeezers out of your kids, but if the offense is great enough, there is a time and place for scared straight.

I'll stop there. Next up, I'll explain my it's *more-no-than-yes* comment.

Takeaway:
- The *yes* part of this question is that certain techniques can be listed, discussed, and taught in a grad school or professional development setting.

Chapter 13:
Special Guest: Curious Teacher – Can Classroom Management be Taught? Part 2

Introduction:
Back to the original question: (Can classroom management be taught in a real classroom setting?)
Here's why I said it's more no than yes.

Classroom management is more art than science.
I'm not saying art can't be taught or that there are no rules, but the rules bend and change as the situation and medium dictates. Techniques that work well for painting with acrylics differ than those for watercolors. Sketching with a pencil and paper is different than drawing digitally. Likewise, each class requires a unique approach.

Why can't classroom management be effectively taught in a classroom setting?
The answer to the question comes from science.

Short answer: There are too many variables.

Long answer (some of those variables in no particular order):
Every class has a unique personality.
This year, I have the Chatty Chaotic Class, the Sweet but Silent Strugglers, the Mostly On-Task All-Stars, and the Social Butterflies.

Even if you've never taught a day in your life but you have been in a public or private school setting, you can probably recognize the types from your past schooling careers.

A teacher who is a parent told me it's similar to raising a child. What works for one will not work for another. This is true for both motivation and discipline.

If I tell the students to work quietly after a test but don't disturb the others, the Chatty Chaos Class will ignore the rules and start talking. I don't think it's a malicious thing, they're just completely thoughtless when it comes to the needs of other test takers.

If I tell the Sweet but Silent Strugglers to get some work done or relax but don't bother anybody, they'll likely play games on their phones.

Because their reactions differ, management techniques must differ.

There's also more than one right answer.
What do you think of as a classroom running smoothly? The immediate answer might be students jotting down notes, but depending on the class, it could be collaborating on a project, building something, designing something, or preparing and conducting interviews.

Teachers have different personalities.
Some people are okay with kids wandering. Others are thoroughly annoyed with wanderers.

If I tried one-two-three eyes on me, my kids would indeed look, but that would also be followed by hysterical laughter.

I can usually get the students to do their lessons, but I also do a lot to get to know them and to work with them on things like deadlines.

I've known teachers who come with two volumes: loud and louder. Other teachers are coaches, so they have that coach mentality. Some kids react well to this, and others do not.

Situations in a classroom are fluid.
You have to be mentally prepared for everything from the kids are climbing on each other to a medical emergency to one's on a desk trying to resuscitate the class skeleton. (Yeah, don't ask.)

Attention spans are short.
Unless it's watching a fun movie or reading a book, people don't typically like sitting still for more than 20 minutes at a time.

Being a student isn't easy. Some personality types like traditional school better than others. Some do better with hands-on things. But to get to the point where one can create, design, and modify to make something better, there still has to be some base knowledge. Bells and whistles are great, but there's still a time and place for direct instruction too.

Often, it comes down to dealing with a handful of students.
And they feed off of each other. Recently, my most lively class had four missing students for one reason or another. Half were gone for a field trip. The entire demeanor of the class changed. It was much more peaceful. Such a thing can't be predicted.

When everybody's present, it's sometimes an hour-long game of whack-a-mole to address the ridiculous things that come out of their mouths.

So ... does anything work for sure?

Be adaptable and fair. Have a good sense of humor. Roll with the weirdness. Set your boundaries and stick with them when those are tested. They will be tested. Find ways to recharge. Have fun.

Takeaways:

- There's no book, no program, no training like pure experience.
- Adaptability is one of the key traits needed for managing a class well.
- A good sense of humor helps.
- Set boundaries, but also be fair and willing to bend if circumstances warrant it.

Chapter 14:
General Opinion: Anatomy of a School Year

Introduction:

Dear Reader,

I thought about calling this Chapter: Why is March a Tough Month for Teachers? But I wanted to talk about more than just the month of March.

Although certain recent years have thrown more curve balls than normal, every year has a general ebb and flow to it.

That's what I want to chat about today.

~Ann

*Note: The exact months for each section are going to vary based on the region. Many schools run August to May. Others run September to June. Private schools may keep their own schedules. When I attended a private school, I fully appreciated the fact that we did not have to adhere to the 180 days of school rule that public schools must abide by.

Second Note: My experience is with older students, so some of the issues faced may be geared to high school.

The hopeful beginning: (first month; ~August/September)
This time is full of promise. Teachers get to meet the new students. Coming directly off of summer, they tend to be better rested than other times of the year. They're ready to get back to business.

Tasks and challenges: Establishing classroom norms, sharing expectations with students, and learning names.

The glow fades: (second half of the first quarter)
Routines should be up and running. Kids are showing their true colors.

Tasks and challenges: Write progress reports, deal with Fall allergy season, chase kids for missing work, and do some parent contact.

Something interesting: The mask mandate made it so that we used less tissues as a class. I think that it was partly in combination with more sick kids—and staff—actually staying home.

The cold mess that is November and December:
Holidays are wonderful. Breaks are wonderful. But the time leading up to significant breaks can be challenging.

Tasks and challenges: Try to get students to focus. Wrap up units at convenient stopping points. Deal with Fall state testing or PSATs or SATs or some other test flavor of the year (if applicable).

Winter:
There's a small window of time just after the winter break wherein things chug along normally. Most of the country (United States) is wrapped in layers of ice or snow or just bracing cold. Even the South gets slapped with chilling temperatures and random snowstorms.

Tasks and challenges: Regain focus after an extended break. Deal with general winter blues in self and students.

The endless month of March:
It's not literally endless, of course, but it sure can seem that way.
Relevant bunny trail ... reasons March is a tough month for teachers:

- There are no major holidays, so unless the school plans something specific, there is a stretch of about 6 weeks with 0 breaks. It's bookended by Presidents' Day weekend and the Spring break, which typically falls around Easter. (Easter is a bit of a moving target since it falls "on the first Sunday after the full moon that is on or after the spring equinox." Thank you, Google, for the handy info.). You don't have to be good at math to understand that a long stretch like 5-6 weeks is stressful to both students and teachers.
- It smells like poop. I'm serious. This may differ per district, but in general, many districts pick sometime in this timeframe to order fertilizer for their spiffy lawns.
- The last rounds of observations are happening, so supervisors can file their reports and districts can figure out who is getting rehired and who is being "non-renewed." (This is a special term that means the teacher will finish the year but does not have a job for the following school term.)
- It's a very long way from the end of the school year.

April. Spring sports. Spring allergies. Banquet season. The End.
After Spring break, there's a definite race to the end of the year.
Tasks and challenges: In a normal year, there's a lot of Spring sports, a resurgence of allergies, banquets, prep for graduation, review for finals, finals, and finally, graduation. By the time summer rolls around, most teachers are happy to see the tail end of certain students, semi-mourning the loss of their superstars, and

so, so ready for some sunshine and two solid months of lack of grading.

Note: There are schools moving to an all-year schedule. I've never been in it, so I can't say much about it besides it's a thing. Some love it. Some hate it.

Takeaways:
- A school year has many sections.
- Teachers look forward to breaks as much or more than students.

Chapter 15:
Teacher Profile: The Overwhelmed First-Year Teacher

Introduction:

Dear Reader,

Every teacher was once a first-year teacher. Depending on their career path, some have multiple first-year experiences in a new place, but there's nothing quite like that initial first-year experience.

Whether you knew it or not, at some point in your school career, you probably had a first-year teacher. Maybe you could see the signs; maybe you couldn't.

~ Ann

A year of firsts:
- First official, on-the-job observations.
- (For some) First real paycheck.
- First time buying school supplies. Pick a favorite style of pen. This is going to be important.

- First set of classroom norms and procedures. So many decisions. Some may be dictated by your school, but most of the time, you get to decide how many students get to leave the room at a time, how long they get to stay gone, whether they need a pass to be in the hallways, and so forth.
- First sit-down chats with the supervisor. These are routine, but they're never super comfortable.
- First run-ins with parents. Nice run-ins are possible, but you are much more likely to encounter ticked off parents.
- First teaching triumphs. This can take many forms. It can be anything from reaching one student to having a lesson plan unfold exactly as you envisioned.
- First time asking a colleague to cover your class for a minute while you use the restroom.
- First classroom management issues. Some classes are naturally easier to deal with than others. Students might have a knack for sensing inexperience, but it's more likely they're always going to press the boundaries. Somebody not used to standing their ground might lose it quickly.
- First time on the other side of the desk. No matter how many years you spent in school, it's different when the responsibility rests upon you.
- (Maybe) First time navigating these strange teaching waters with a co-teacher. I've been privileged to work with several wonderful co-teachers, but it's always possible you have a personality conflict or difference of opinion on how to handle certain situations.
- First time trying to find the balance between home and school life. There's no question that teaching is a job that comes home with you. Unpaid hours are part and parcel of the package deal we signed up for. Balance is achievable but not always easy first round.

- First time facing the prospect of planning for a substitute teacher to take over for the day. It's daunting. There's a surprising amount of things to do to take a day off.
- First time buying school apparel from one of countless fundraisers.
- First time attending high school sports games as a spectator simply to support your kids. Same goes for school plays and concerts. They love to see teachers there, and it's always interesting to see kids in a setting that's not a normal classroom.

Things first-year teachers do (that others may not):
- Spend a lot of time lesson planning. Every teacher must lesson plan according to whatever outline the supervisor wants, but the first year is the worst for this because a) you probably don't have a lot of premade/past lessons to pull from and b) you're probably about 2 days ahead of the kids.
- Fret about grading things right away. First-year teachers tend to be wired to want to impress, so there is a higher chance they will take home stuff to grade at night and over weekends.
- Freak out about observations. This largely depends on one's personality. Some people get nervous every single time for decades. Every first experience has the potential to be uncomfortable simply because of the many unknowns.
- Sort through an inordinate amount of conflicting advice. People want to help, but every experience is different. Some things are different beasts when defined inside the safe space of a training ground and in a live situation.
- Attend a lot of professional development and conferences. Some teachers really love to stretch themselves for the knowledge. The glow of attending conferences fades for

some but not all.

What to do when you encounter a first-year teacher:
- Encourage where possible.
- Listen to their concerns and frustrations.
- Feed them chocolate (unless they are allergic).
- Give a sturdy travel mug because they're going to need it.

Takeaways:
- Teaching is a hard but rewarding career, but first-year teaching is typically its own special brand of new and terrifying experiences all rolled up into one 10-month stretch.
- If you encounter a first-year teacher, be nice to them.

Chapter 16:
General Opinion: To Care or Not to Care about Dress Code?

Introduction:

Dear Reader,

I know it's way more common to have a uniform across the pond, but in the United States, generally only certain private schools have uniforms for the students.

In a way, having a uniform would help with dress code issues, but I don't think it would completely solve the problems because they're usually not about clothes at all.

Most public schools have a dress code, but it rarely gets officially enforced.

Teachers also have a dress code to abide by.

That's what I want to chat about today.

~Ann

What's in a dress code?

I'll be the first to admit that I haven't read hundreds of dress codes, but the few I have read usually have a few things in common. They usually say something about promoting adult-only stuff such as beer, cigarettes, etc. Some touch on avoiding politics, though typically common sense prevails here.

Why even have dress codes?

- To keep the peace.
- To minimize distractions.
- To preserve the professional atmosphere.

What leads kids to break dress codes?

- Kids trying to fit in.
- Kids trying to one-up the competition.
- Kids testing boundaries with the school or parents.
- Different parental definitions of what constitutes okay clothes.
- Kids not really thinking what they do, say, or wear has any meaning or ramifications.

Why is the dress code rarely enforced?

- It's a relatively minor thing that can usually be addressed informally.
- Most people don't want to step on an emotional landmine without any backup.
- If an administrator or teacher is of the opposite gender than the student in question, there's the potential for kicking over a whole tub of explosive crap.
- Administration might give the student a talking-to and parents might take an interest, but most likely anybody who says something gets yelled at or hears a toothless yes-we'll-speak-with-him/her.

How have things changed since the pandemic?

I can only speak from my experience, but I am noticing more students wearing sweatpants and pajama pants around the high school.

While there's nothing inherently wrong with wearing sleepwear to school, I wouldn't recommend it either.

What's wrong with comfortable or stylish (but super skimpy) clothes?

In general, nothing. But there is a time and place for everything. One shouldn't dress like they're attending a nightclub or wild party if they're headed to school.

Students already have a lot of distractions to deal with. (I think distractions will be its own topic later.)

Have you ever heard the phrase *the clothes make the man*?

The saying has two meanings. (Thank you, Google, for the definitions).

On the surface, it means that people judge one based on what you wear. That's definitely true. From a peer perspective, I suspect that's the entire reason students dress a certain way.

They want to enhance and emphasize a particular part of their personality to manipulate the way others perceive them.

Below the surface, it also means that there's a mindset attached to certain clothes. This is also true.

Sweatpants and casual sleepwear are certainly more comfortable, but they're also a mixed signal. I'm not saying we want students on edge in school, but for many, this is their job. It pays in praise and grades and the occasional lollipop. They should come dressed ready to do that job.

What is the teacher dress code?

I'm sure it's defined somewhere in the employee handbook.

My interpretation of what is likely a long-winded, formally worded section on dos and don'ts is: don't look like a slob.

I can say that professional dress is factored into some evaluation systems.

Side note: There are heated debates over showing tattoos. Nobody I know has personally had a problem with having or not having tattoos, but one colleague waited until she earned tenure before letting her tattoos show.

Second side note: I asked a homeschooling parent if her kids are allowed to do school in their PJs. She said no. (I am aware this isn't proof of what I'm saying. I haven't asked enough people to qualify it as a study, but I suspect these views are not radically unique.)

I'm one of those people who shower and change immediately when I get home. I get the allure of comfy stuff.

Takeaway:

- Not so long ago, the bedroom was the classroom. Now that we get to return to a real classroom, there should be some mental separation between home and school. Dressing the part helps.

Chapter 17:
Special Guest: A Veteran Homeschooler Answers Some of my Burning Questions

Introduction:
Dear Reader,

My experience rests mainly in public schools, so I'm excited to bring you a different perspective today.

I recently got to hear from a Veteran Homeschooler—both as a student and as a parent—who was willing to answer some questions about how that system works.

~Ann

What is a co-op?
Of course, I Googled it to be sure I had the definition right in my head. (I did.) It's a group of families who get together to meet for a common goal.

Are there different kinds of co-ops? How do they function?

The way co-ops are run depends on the families involved. The most common format I have encountered is a group of families agreeing to meet regularly (once a week, every other week, or once a month).

During the time they meet, the parents teach classes on different subjects, and the students choose which classes to be part of.

Inner musings:

That's interesting. I'm so used to students being locked into a certain schedule for a marking period, a semester, or an entire year. I don't know if that's true freedom or a terrifying lack of structure.

What's the second form of co-op?

Another form of this is when the families pool their resources to pay a tutor for a specific topic. Some homeschool groups get together and go on field trips together. Others just have playdates.

Which kind do you have experience with?

The one I participated in when I was growing up was called a homeschool group. We ate lunch together once a week.

We occasionally went on field trips together, but mostly the kids played and/or the parents organized activities together like a science fair, gingerbread house making, guest speakers, etc.

As a pre-teen, I organized plays with the younger kids and started a coloring club. Every week we did presentations for the group.

Do all homeschool kids join a co-op?

No. The group my kids currently participate in is called Classical Conversations, which isn't a co-op. It is more of a curriculum that we follow with other families. Once a week, we gather and go over new material that we are going to study over the course of the coming week.

The students meet weekly for community day.

What happens during community day?

For the younger ages, it includes history, math, science with weekly science experiments, fine arts, geography, English grammar, Latin, and presentations. The students do 2-to-3-minute presentations to their classmates on various topics.

For the older grades, which includes junior high through high school, the students spend community day discussing what they have learned during the school week, apply it to their world view, go over new information, and challenge each other to excel further under the oversight of a tutor.

There is a focus on the Socratic Method, especially in the older grades. In Junior High, students do a science fair and a mock trial. In High School, they participate in formal debates, memorize and present long passages of literature, and collaborate in other large, organized events each year.

What happens when you're not attending co-op or some other organized group community day?

During the rest of the school week, the individual families work through the material at home, so they are ready to digest new material the next community day.

My response:

Thanks for taking the time to share your insights into this different way of doing school.

I love that there's an emphasis on general socialization, presenting one's findings, participating in discussions, and even defending one's position.

It sounds like homeschooling can be a great option, but I can also understand why it's not an option for a lot of families.
That's a lot of responsibility for the parents.

I imagine student success depends largely on self-motivation. The idea of being able to move through study materials at one's own pace has a lot of appeal, but I can also easily picture there being *classroom management* issues with certain kids just based on their personalities.

Takeaways:
- I'm glad to hear homeschooling works out well for some families.

The other thing I really enjoy about the description of homeschool is that playdates are a part of it. I think it's too easy for kids (and folks in general) to see school as this arduous thing that just needs to be done, rather than an opportunity to grow and learn and play.

Chapter 18:
Administrator Profile: The Conflict Avoider and Issue Amplifier

Introduction:

Dear Reader,

Disclaimer: I fully intend to write about all manner of teachers, students, administrators, and parents. Some depictions will be flattering, and some will not. I promised to be honest. This is in no way admin-bashing. They are one of the 4 pillar stakeholders for any school.

(The 5th is staff like maintenance and secretaries. They are vital too, but typically, people don't hold super strong opinions about them.)

Like any profession, there are some administrators who are very good at their jobs and others who are not. Today, I'd like to discuss the administrator who really hates conflict and/or chooses very small things to amplify.

~Ann

Conflict is never easy.

I understand the instinct to avoid conflict. Within reason, that's how I function. I'd rather be inconvenienced than step into a conflict. However, there are times where conflict is inevitable, and teachers and administrators need to step up and enter the fray.

In those cases, administrators get paid the big bucks because handling those fires is their job. To say one thing and do another is confusing and frustrating for everyone involved.

Everybody has something they're passionate about.

It just happens that sometimes people choose odd battles to wage.

What if an administrator says one thing and does another?

Example 1:

Once upon a time, there was a science supervisor who obsessed over lab safety. She observed a teacher do a lesson where the students were handling salt water and ice in glass beakers. The teacher had not made a big deal out of forcing the students to wear safety goggles because the substances inside are inherently harmless household chemicals.

Basically, the supervisor had an internal meltdown. She spoke with the teacher. He acknowledged the advice and thought everything was fine. Fast forward a little while, he gets called by the principal to chat about goggles and lab safety.

My response to Example 1:

Lab safety is indeed important. There are always horror stories of things going wrong in a lab and leading to injuries. That's not the point.

The point is that clearly, the supervisor was bothered by the lack of safety goggles. Nobody is faulting her for that. The problem is the breakdown in communication. She indicated things are fine, but then, she also chose to escalate the issue by taking it up the chain of command.

What if an administrator makes mountains from molehills?
Example 2:
Once upon a different time, there was a supervisor who saw a teacher show students both good and bad examples of projects. Fearing a potential HIB (harassment, intimidation, and bullying) incident, said supervisor brought it up with the teacher.

The teacher pointed out that with the student group in question, it's more likely the kid who turned in the thing used as a good example would be targeted.

My response to Example 2:
I think the supervisor was probably stretching for something to nitpick here, but I guess the way to avoid such things is to give examples from previous years. That's not always possible, but the likelihood of students knowing who made what at that point goes down.

Most kids won't care one way or the other. The teacher had a valid point though that criticism could go either way.

Example 3:
Once upon yet another time, there was a supervisor who scolded a teacher for kids having their phones out.

My response to Example 3:
At the high school level, phones can be a legitimate concern. How teachers respond to the problem varies. When possible, the issue is addressed, usually by a request to put the phone away. However, it can be like playing nine games of whack-a-mole simultaneously to keep telling kids to put their phones away, so it's not something every teacher attends to every second of the class. If they did, nothing would get done. Ever.

Some students are genuine phone addicts with little to no impulse control. Getting them to sit for 2 minutes straight is a feat. So, fighting a continual battle about their phones sometimes isn't top priority.

I suppose the supervisor has the prerogative to address what she wants, but it sounds like a situation where there are probably bigger fish to fry.

Why would phones potentially be low priority for classroom management issues?

An isolated student on his or her phone is usually only sabotaging their own learning opportunities. The issues that require more direct intervention are those that distract several students or the entire classroom.

Personal story:

During my first year of teaching, I remember crying because I was so frustrated that the things being raised as points of conflict were so insignificant and stupid like kids having gum in class.

Why is this important?

Both issues—saying one thing, doing another and fighting over small stuff—undermines the confidence teachers have in their administrators. This lack of confidence makes both types of jobs more difficult to execute and messes with the workplace morale.

Takeaways:

- No matter who you are and what you do, being honest in your dealings with people is usually the way to go. Not saying be blunt to the point of rude, but if something bothers you, raise it with the person directly.
- Conflict's not easy, but if that's your job, you're going to have to deal with it at some point. Letting things fester just makes it messier when they finally explode.
- Administrators have a lot to do. Picking fights with teachers over little things seems counterproductive.

Chapter 19:
Special Guest: Concerned Parent Feeling Ignored – Conflicts with Teachers

Introduction:
Dear Reader,

Most concerns you'll read about in the series are from a teacher's perspective because that's who I have the most contact with.

That's why I'm thrilled to be able to bring you a parent concern today.

~Ann

The problem:
Dear Ann,

What do you do when it is obvious that you (as a parent) can't see eye to eye with a teacher?

I kept explaining to my son's teacher that he is very smart. Gifted smart. So, he was bored in her class.

The very first week of Kindergarten I told her that he knows every one of the words she has listed for the end of the year test.

I think she thought I was being dramatic or exaggerating because my son has a bit of an attitude.

I asked for more difficult work on several occasions, and she just gave us more worksheets at Pre-K to Kindergarten level.

We were doing live stream classes because of Covid and when she was getting on him about staying on task, he called her boring. She did not take it well.

I stuck it out but had to have a come-to-Jesus meeting with the principal, who almost switched my son's classes due to the conflict.

~Concerned Parent (Feeling Ignored)

My response:
Dear Feeling Ignored,

Ironically, you were ignored twice. This one was completely my fault. I am so, so sorry it took me this long to get this on the schedule. (The concern got shuffled onto a version of the form I stopped checking.)

I will talk about your situation, which sounds like a combination of things, but I'd also like to discuss some other concerns parents usually raise.

Potential points of conflict (most common issues parents raise with teachers):
The dos:
- Student interactions with peers
- Student grades, assignments, class difficulty, workload

- Student interactions with the teacher (feeling picked on or singled out)

My response to student interactions with each other:

Hopefully, these explanations and comments don't come across as defensive.

There's a general (very reasonable) expectation that teachers establish a safe learning environment that caters to every student. That said, it's impossible to monitor and correct every conversation happening in the room.

Side note: I was once asked to keep certain students away from each other because they had come to blows over something or other earlier in the day. (The students in question are high school boys.) Short of tying them up in opposite corners, which is frowned upon, that's an impossible request. Their seats were apart from each other, but students move about the classroom for various reasons.

If a parent raised such a concern with me, I would likely promise to attempt to be on the lookout for whatever they wanted, but full promises of prevention are impossible to give.

My response to grade and assignment issues:

I'm sure I'll expand on this later, but there's a misconception that teachers *give* students grades. If the system is working correctly, teachers provide ways for students to earn grades, students do assignments, and teachers evaluate the work to assign grade values to the things handed in.

There are life situations that make it so that dropping certain things is advisable, but most of the responsibility for grades earned should rest upon the students.

The fails-to-dos:

- Teacher is not addressing student conflicts
- Teacher is not available to help the student

- Teacher is failing to manage a student's behaviors well
- Teacher is not helping the student reach their full potential

The current situation sounds like a combination of the last two from the second list.

Recap: A student is off-task because he already knows the material. When the teacher tried to redirect him, he called her boring. A few things escalated and the mother ended up talking with the principal.

My response to the situation raised by Feeling Ignored:

First, I'll admit I laughed at what your son said. Kids are brutally honest. On the other hand, I can also see why his teacher didn't take that well. Nobody likes being called out on something—true or not—especially by a small child.

Can't recall if anybody has ever told me to my face that my class is boring, but I'm sure plenty have thought it over the years. It can be an it's-not-you-it's-me situation. My students are high schoolers. The odds of my subject being the favorite of everyone is zip. That's just human nature. There's a reason I don't teach other subjects. (Most of them were deadly boring when I was a student, and I like me enough to spare me.)

People react differently. Even if a student did tell me class is boring, my response would be something along the lines of: So? Get back to work. If you don't do enough of the work, you fail. If you fail, you have to redo this class in summer school or next year, and newsflash, you don't seem to be having a great time now. Why would you want the prospect of doing it again?

There's a little more to this story, but I'm going to split it into a separate entry on gifted children.

For now, let's just cut to the conclusion. What do you do if you find yourself in a similar situation?

Standard conflict management. Take it up with the teacher. If that doesn't solve the problem, escalate to guidance and the supervisor or principal.

Takeaway:

- In my humble opinion, the mother did things right, even though the teacher in me cringes at any parent-principal conversations revolving around what happens in a classroom.

Chapter 20:
Special Guest: Concerned High School Teacher – The Gift of Failure

Introduction:

Dear Reader,

Can you tell teachers are worried about the general state of schools? Okay, so, the numbers of concerns raised thus far is small, but I'm already detecting some themes.

Let's hear from a Concerned High School Teacher. The person didn't leave me a real name or email address, but that merely reinforces the idea that it's a concern shared by many.

I can guess from context this person teaches English Language Arts (probably to high schoolers).

I think the person referred to themselves as Head Shaker because that's probably what was happening while the person filled in the form. The slightly desperate, slightly frustrated tone came through clearly enough.

~Ann

Dear Ann,

My concern is about students' lack of ability to try and fail, and their lack of ability to work.

I've got the kids that don't shut up, of course, but 85+% of my students won't dare venture a guess when I ask a question unless I call them out specifically. Even if it's a question I've already given the answer to twice.

My guess is they don't want to fail, but failure is just part of the process.

Then, there are essays.

You'd think a two-page essay assignment was a demand to handwrite the dictionary. I tell them how essays worked when I was in school—two to five pages per trimester in each of my humanities classes—totaling up to eighteen a year. Not that it helps. They still think two pages is equivalent to a doctoral thesis. Sure, I know the pandemic threw them for a loop. It threw us all for a loop. But how did we get here, and more importantly, how do we get back?

Particularly when having high standards is seen as a fault by administration—*"You're failing too many kids"* becomes a black mark against the teacher—rather than a good thing?

~Concerned High School Teacher (Head Shaker)

My response:
Dear Head Shaker,

Thank you for sharing. You raise many excellent points.

If I'm reading your concerns correctly, they are three-fold: kids fear to fail, kids don't want to work, and administration fears failure makes them look bad. As a result, the administrators press the teachers to magically make it so that no student fails.

Student fear of failure:

I thought about your statement in terms of my students, and I believe your number is spot-on. In a class of roughly twenty students, I can expect about three of them to offer answers. If called upon, most of the others can give the answer. They just don't want to either because of laziness or a fear of offering an incorrect answer.

Possible solutions:

- Perhaps we have a perception problem. Many students love video games and sports. There, they understand that failure is part of the process. Maybe they need that perspective.
- Gamification is a thing that works for some people, but only if the teacher has a genuine love of that sort of thing.
- I'm a fan of direct, so I'd probably try to take the sting out of wrong answers.
- If you really want to get radical, change the format of the class so it's more of a student discussion. This only works for certain lessons.
- Participation points might motivate some.
- Provide alternate ways to answer, like on paper that nobody but the kid can see.
- Outright bribery – answer five questions in a class and claim a lollipop, that sort of thing.

Student fear of work (especially essays):

This too might be a perception problem. The word essay embodies the idea of work, and hard work at that. These entries and musings are essentially 600-900-word essays, but I don't really think of them that way. It's more like having short conversations with friends, colleagues, and strangers.

Possible solution:

Try proving that the length is not the issue. By that, before you introduce the first official essay you wanted them to do, have the students free write something they're passionate about. It's essentially a personal essay about themselves, a sports team they like, a talent they have, etc., but don't mention the dreaded e-word. Then, have them throw it into a word counter and see how many words they wrote in a certain amount of time.

Administrators fearing that failure makes them look bad:

I'm not sure there's a way to alter administrators' views of failure. As much as we like to think of the individual students and their needs, by the time the reports reach the admin level, there are no faces, only names and numbers of failures. Well, until a parent of a failing student pitches a fit. Then, you have a name.

Thoughts on the problem:

This is wider than administration. There's an emphasis on standardized tests to prove student readiness to face the wider world. That creates an obsession with showing a certain kind of proficiency. It creates a black and white world of pass/fail.

The administration gets flak if the numbers don't look good, so they turn around and pressure teachers to make the numbers look good, regardless of the amount of comprehension happening in the students.

Possible solutions:

- How much energy do you have? You can choose the grassroots method of educating people from the ground up, or you could join the dark side (administration or school governance) and fight the issue from there.
- On a personal level, play the perceptions game. Make it so that students must actively try to fail. That way, if admin comes after you, you can show the students had every opportunity to pass and chose not to do so.

Takeaways:

- As this teacher mentioned, failure is a part of the process.
- Let's try to find ways to make failure less frightening. Just because one loses a game doesn't mean they are a loser in the full context of that word.

Chapter 21:
Special Guest: Feeling Ignored Raises Another Parent Concern – Gifted Students

Introduction:

Dear Reader,

Today, we welcome back Feeling Ignored.

I'll summarize for those who either skipped that Chapter or read it a while ago.

Scenario Summary:

Incident 1:

Feeling Ignored's child was bored in his Kindergarten class because he already knew the material. He called the teacher boring, and she took offense to the statement.

Incident 2:

Feeling Ignored wanted to get her child tested for being gifted. The teacher also took offense to what she saw as parent meddling, so she sent a scathing email to the mother.

What happened:

The principal had to be brought in for conflict resolution. She apologized for the email and offered to have Feeling Ignored's son transferred to a new class since the teacher and parent were not seeing eye-to-eye on the level of his education.

~Ann

Dear Ann,

We ended up not changing classrooms. I told my son we have to deal with difficult people throughout our whole lives, and we need to find a way to work things out.

After the principal got involved, things smoothed out, but I hated that it had to come to that.

Only thing I can add is that now my son is in gifted classes. Because there aren't many gifted students his age, he is in class with 3rd graders. I feel vindicated in that sense but once again, I hate that it took months of struggling with the school to get to this point.

The teacher made several comments that literally made me feel like a bad mom for working.

On top of the work the teacher gave, I added some 1st grader homework to the mix to make sure my son stayed on top. I just wish there had been a better way for the two of us to have communicated early on.

Or maybe I should have switched classes.

Or maybe I am delusional in thinking that most of schoolwork is done in school. I never imagined that as a parent I would have to spend 20-30 hours a week helping my son with extra schoolwork. I know my parents didn't.

Ann Y. Mouse

~Feeling Ignored

My response:
Feeling Ignored's advice to her son was excellent. There are difficult people to deal with in all aspects of life.

Even though I'm not an elementary teacher, I can understand the defensive stance taken by the teacher in this situation. When one works hard to prepare what most of the students need, it's vexing to be told it's not good enough for one particular child.

The story has a happy ending, but there was a lot of conflict along the way.

Could the conflict have been avoided?
Maybe, but hindsight is always perfect.

Since I wasn't involved with the situation, I don't know all the sources of conflict. It sounds like there was a disconnect between what Feeling Ignored felt would be an acceptable Kindergarten education and what the teacher had prepared to present the class.

Clear communication is certainly important, but it's not a foolproof plan.

It sounds like Feeling Ignored knew what her son needed, so why didn't the teacher just get the kid more advanced work?
Teachers—including myself—get touchy when parents offer suggestions on curriculum adjustments. This happens for two reasons. 1) Most of the time, they don't know what they're talking about, and 2) it comes across as a vote of no confidence.

The teaching profession has a lot of built-in back seat drivers, so adding one more (usually incompetent) comes across as insulting.

A note about professionalism:
Oh, the stories I could tell you about what I'd wanted to say to

parents. Perhaps I will, but the difference is that anonymity takes the sting out of feeling targeted.

I have no idea what the teacher said to Feeling Ignored in the email that the principal ended up apologizing for. This is why teachers need teacher buddies to vent to and check emails before they're sent into cyberspace.

Composing an articulate email that presents one's position without insulting the other party is time consuming. It also takes energy. Never email in anger.

Would a class switch have helped?

It's hard to tell, and very likely that a class switch would only have changed the shade of the problem without solving anything because the heart of the matter was the Kindergarten work was too easy.

The best solution would probably have been to homeschool her son, but as Feeling Ignored mentioned, this wasn't an option. She needed to work. Public schools exist to serve the community because a lot of families need multiple sources of income.

To the idea that most of the schoolwork is done in school ...

It can be this way, but that mostly depends on the teacher's personal philosophy about homework.

I don't give a lot of homework. Mostly, if my students have homework, it's because they neglected to use their time wisely in class.

Some people give homework because it's expected (even mandated) by the school. This is especially true in the lower grades as they strive to prepare students for middle school and high school workloads.

I've even heard of things like if a kid is in this grade they should receive x amount of minutes of homework per subject.

Feeling Ignored did a lot of extra work to make sure her son had enough to do at home to stay ahead of his peers. That's a noble sacrifice she made for her child. (On the flip side, asking a teacher to do that much additional work to reach one child can be difficult to handle.)

Takeaways:
- Emails should not be sent in the heat of the moment, any moment.

We hear a lot more about kids who are falling behind, but kids who are well ahead of their peers also require extra attention and work. Who that work falls to can be a point of contention.

Chapter 22:
Student Profile: The Phone Addict

Introduction:

Dear Reader,

Students fit many different profiles depending on the day (or hour), but there's usually one or two names that pop into mind if somebody mentions a kid who wanders, is constantly on the phone, or leaves the classroom every day.

If you're beyond high school, think of what label your teachers would have given you.

Disclaimer: As with any of these profiles, I am highlighting one aspect of the student's behavior to discuss the issue.

Today's student profile topic is The Phone Addict.

~Ann

Note: Some schools have policies that limit student phone use, but for the purpose of discussion, I'm assuming that the issue has been left to teacher discretion. This is very common anyway since most administrators don't like being the *bad guy* when it comes to anything.

Certain lower elementary grades may not have a phone problem. I'm not sure what the current age is where parent start letting their kids have a cell phone.

I imagine it's a problem from middle school on.

When did it become a problem for schools to deal with?

Those who have been teaching a while got to see the phenomenon happen. I can't recall if it was problematic when I first started out. Kids had cell phones, but I think the difference is that they didn't do all that much besides access email, send text messages, and occasionally take a clunky photo. Today, cell phones are gaming devices, movie screens, music players, and an easy way to access social media.

Phones are needed for emergencies.

But there was a blessed time before every child had a cell phone.

I'm texting my mom ...

Is still a terrible excuse. Always has been, always will be. If a student needs to talk to his or her parent, simply asking for permission to do so is fine. These are exceptions, not the rule.

To be fair to the students, most middle-class Americans are phone addicts.

If you go to any restaurant, mall, coffee shop, or other public location, you'd have an easier time of counting people not on their phones.

I rarely go anywhere without my phone.

The difference is that I can put it down if necessary.

Most kids have a phone.

And when given time at the end of class, most will access their devices. Those aren't the kids we're talking about.

How do you identify phone addicts?

- Student phone addicts make attempts to be sneaky.
- The screen glows, so hiding it on their laps makes the underside of the desk glow too.
- They hide it in their calculators even when such things aren't being used in class.
- They hide it behind their computers (if they have one).
- They may also have the phone out, put it away, then have it out again two seconds later.

When the phone is addressed the second, third, or fourth time, they either look at the teacher with annoyance or innocence.

I think some of them genuinely forget they were asked to put it away a few minutes (or seconds) prior.

Did the pandemic make things worse?

Probably. I don't recall there being quite so many kids who try to have an AirPod or other wireless headphone in while class is happening in the pre-pandemic years. However, that could also be a coincidence of the technology becoming more prevalent during the same years as the Covid craze.

What can be done to save The Phone Addict from themselves?
Possible solutions:

- Phone jail – I have seen people have some success with this. It's most commonly a plastic or cloth shoe holder that's draped over the door or a plastic bin. Students drop off their phones at the beginning of class and claim it on the way out.

- Just keep yelling – I definitely wrote that with Dory in my head singing it. It's not really yelling. It's more like a constant drip request. Most will eventually get the point.
- Remove the device – Ask the phone addict to put the phone on the teacher's desk. If they're worried about it, the device could also be placed in a drawer behind the teacher's desk. Most can't stand to have it out of sight that long, so they choose to leave it on the desk.
- Use phone time as a reward for reaching a certain class or daily goal. I always have a set amount of things I know we should be able to get to. All additional time belongs to the students to use as they please. Inevitably, it's phone time. Occasionally, I strive to get them to have a real conversation with each other, but most of the time, I'm content to let them disappear into their anti-social social media musings.

Please note: This third method has worked reasonably well for me, but if you're a teacher, you'd have to check the rules of your school to see if you're allowed to take phones away.

If they push back, remind the students that you are trying to save them from themselves. It's not forever, and there's a time and place for everything. The middle of class isn't the best time to be watching a personal movie, messaging friends, or checking up on your social media.

If parents complain, ask them for their suggestions. Compromise. If a request to keep the phone in a zipped part of the child's backpack will work, go with it. The top of the desk is a terrible place because it will inevitably be in their hands thirty seconds later.

Takeaways:
- Phones are a problem that won't go away for a while.

- Somehow, seek to separate the child from the device for that brief time when class is happening.
- Phones are a privilege and a safety blanket. Having them close but inaccessible should be a decent compromise.

Chapter 23:
Special Guest: A Teen Services Librarian's Journey

Introduction:

Dear Reader,

I recently had the chance to talk with a Teen Services Librarian who happened to mention she taught English Language Arts once upon a very short time.

Being the curious critter I am, I had to ask what brought her into and out of the teaching world.

She provided a very thorough, awesome answer.

~Ann

Dear Ann,

Wow, you asked a loaded question for me.

(My question was basically two-fold: Why did you start teaching, and why did you stop teaching?)
I should probably preface my answer by saying, I never really wanted to be a teacher.

I had degrees in English, Psychology, and was just finishing up my MFA (Masters of Fine Arts) in Creative Writing when I realized I couldn't get a job with any of those degrees.

I was introduced to the idea of being a school librarian because you wouldn't have to teach, but you'd still get your summers off to write. So, I decided to go down that career path, only to discover that to be a school librarian, not only do you need your MLS (Master's in Library Science), but you need to be a certified teacher and to have been a teacher of record for three years. (These were/are the requirement for Texas, where I'm from.)

So, I entered an alternative certification program and was installed in a 9th grade English classroom where I taught for one year. I succeeded in getting my teacher's certification, but I knew that I could not continue teaching for the three years it would take to qualify me to be a school librarian.

So, I decided, hell, I'll just be a regular librarian, and went and got my MLS with a specialty in Young Adult Services.

Dare I ask what drove you from teaching?
Here is why I knew I couldn't keep teaching and what teaching helped me uncover within myself.

1. I am easily bored by repetition. First period was my guinea pig for new lessons, I used my second period which was planning to tweak, third period got the better lesson, and by fifth period I was a pro and had conquered the lesson ... only to have to do it for two more periods before I would then have to stay after to lead tutoring sessions. I was eternally bored.

2. My 6th period class was awful.

3. Administration was the devil. They made us stop teaching according to the Texas State lesson plans and do testing drills out of workbooks for eight weeks. They suspended kids who they thought would fail the state test a week before we gave them out. They even sabotaged a teacher across the hall from me because they didn't like her and openly admitted to it.

4. School started at 7:00 am, meaning I had to be up at 5:30. I abhor early. Detest it with every fiber of my being.

5. I worked too much. I had no free time, and as a result, I never wrote. (And wasn't I doing this to write?)

That's quite the list. You also mentioned things you learned from the experience. Would you mind sharing them?

Here's why I'm glad I taught:

1. I became a better public speaker. I got over myself in front of large crowds and learned to just say what needed to be said.

2. I learned how to organize lessons and tasks, which others marvel at when it comes to planning and running programs.

3. I had an epiphany. I really liked kids, especially teenagers. I didn't know that before. I was inspired to become a Teen Services Librarian to work with teens. I enjoyed listening to them talk and offering them guidance and being that outside adult they could trust to help them. I did want to work with them, but only when it came to the fun, optional stuff. No parents, no administration, no pressure. Just, what do you want to do today, guys? Let's have fun.

My response:

That's quite the experience. I'm glad you found a position that you enjoy relatively quickly.

The first year of teaching is usually the worst, but it also sounds like your school administration was getting creative with making themselves look good in terms of the passing numbers.

Everybody has a proverbial 6th period. (That's the awful one a teacher ends up dreading because they suck the energy out of you.) To be fair, it's usually not every kid, just a few, select, very high maintenance members who turn the joint into a circus by showing up and being their hot-mess selves.

Takeaways:
- Teaching isn't the right job for everyone, but it's a powerful learning experience.
- There are other jobs that allow one to interact with teens in a more relaxed setting than a classroom.

Chapter 24:
Special Guest: Curious Teacher –
Inappropriate Use of Technology

Introduction:

Dear Ann,

One of my students has turned into a nightmare for the technology department.

We use a program that allows us to monitor student activity on their school Chromebooks. My co-teacher often has it running so we can close tabs and see what students are up to.

Although there are many incidents I could speak of, I'll just mention that once he was caught on a hacking site messing with things on my Google classroom page.

My co-teacher grabbed the relevant screenshots, and we reported the incident to school administrators. I believe he was pulled out of a class to get a lecture on appropriate use of technology, but that's about it.

I guess my main question is: how should we address student misuse of technology (Chromebooks, phones, and so forth)?

~Curious Teacher

My response:
Dear Curious Teacher,

I'm sorry to hear you've had a lot of trouble with this one student. I'm sure there are many people in that position who don't have a program to monitor the behavior or who just don't happen to be looking at the right place at the right time.

Before I get to possible solutions, I'm going to admit to some curiosity too. After writing up the recent article about student phone addictions, I did a very small, informal survey of some teachers.

~Ann

The question was: **When are cell phones a problem in your classroom?**
(I think it also got interpreted as: at which grade level do phones become problematic and when do kids get cell phones?)

The results were very interesting.

Many said students are getting cell phones sometime in elementary school. Two even said Pre-K! I feel like a dinosaur admitting that cell phones weren't a thing when I was that age, but it's true.

Side note: I've recently seen a baby with a toy that looked like a cell phone. While adorable, I'm not sure we want to walk that crazy road. Then again, I guess the kid is going to see the mother's cell phone and want to play. They're a part of life at this point.

The middle school arena feedback varied more than the elementary information. The consensus was that students had cell phones by 6th grade, but it didn't become truly problematic until about 7th and 8th grade.

One teacher admitted that part of the success was full backing from administration and parents to take phones away and send them to the office.

By high school, there was agreement that phones are already a huge problem. Teacher tactics differed from doing nothing to launching constant, nagging reminders.

One person said they have a conversation with the high school kids about employability and time management. That's an awesome idea.

While I like the idea of putting the responsibility on students' shoulders, mine have been making habitually bad decisions. I do not trust them with their phones. Oh, they still sneak it, but that also means if they're busy trying to sneak their phone, they tend to be up to less other mischief in the room.

Possible solutions to the tech nightmare problem:
While I don't have huge hopes for Curious Teacher's student reforming on his own, there are some tidbits from the phone conversation that might be applicable.

As with normal teaching, a wide array of tactics should be employed regularly for best effect.

- Talk to students about responsible use of technology. One signature on a piece of paper or a form at the beginning of the year isn't enough. We all (parents, teachers, students) know that repetition is necessary in every other part of teaching. I suspect this issue is no different.
- Try to get parent and administration backing early. Good communication can help. You have no control over either party but being proactive can help.
- Let students risk failure in little ways (ones you can give them the means to recover from if they reform their errant ways). Failure is never comfortable, but kids will only be

kids so long. Schools are a safe place to fail enough to learn important life lessons.

- Remove the distraction, be it phone or computer or smart watch. You will likely need clearance to do so.

Reminders when it comes to tech fights:

- Remember to protect yourself and the students. We live and work in scary times. Document the heck out of everything.
- Do what's best for your mental wellbeing too. If you have the time and energy to fight the phone and computer games battle, do it. If you don't, monitor as best you can, but put more emphasis on students self-monitoring.

Takeaways (tactics to try):

- Bring up acceptable use multiple times.
- Work with parents and administrators if possible. Take cues from those parties as to which methods might work.
- If it's particularly hard for one student to stay on task, ask for permission to do more things with pen and paper.

Chapter 25:
Parent or Guardian Profile:
The Administrative Assistant

Introduction:

Dear Reader,

As with any of these profiles, there's the potential for somebody to see too much of themselves in it and get offended.

In deference to this fact, I'm going to start with one that's close to neutral in terms of its ability to tick people off if they have these tendencies.

Parents naturally start out doing everything for their child because their kid is too young to self-advocate.

When they're very young, it's easy to make the decision to do stuff like contact teachers if problems arise. As children enter middle school or high school, they should begin handling some things on their own.

Please note: I'm a high school teacher. By the time students reach this level, the vast majority of them should be self-advocating.

Some personality types have no problem taking things on themselves, and others need to be prompted to do so.

There are always exceptions, whether from mental capacity or maturity, but you won't know if your child is capable of writing emails or setting up appointments if you don't let them try.

~Ann

Who is the Administrative Assistant Parent? (How would teachers recognize one?)

In my experience, this is a parent who emails the teacher to set up extra help sessions, contact about pending or recent absences, or express grade concerns.

There are good times to call or email a particular teacher. (I like email, but I think there are still a few who prefer phones.)

In fact, more communication would be nicer in many cases.

- If your child is ill, let teachers know.
- If something catastrophic has happened in your child's life – they lost a friend, are dealing with cancer treatments, is watching a sibling struggle with something, lost their dog, etc.
- If you're seeing great struggles at home with one subject.

For the record, most parent-initiated contact isn't all that comfortable.

So, it might be good to reach out with small words of encouragement or greetings. The point is that bridge-building goes both ways.

What does self-advocating look like?

It's mostly teacher email contact like ...

- I missed class, what do I have to do?
- I missed a test, when can I make it up?

- I'm having trouble, do you have extra help?

Side note about extra help.
The morning of a test or quiz is not the best time for extra help. Could it help? Sure. But it's most likely not enough to cover for two weeks of inattention in class. Learning takes time.

Emailing is not a perfect system.
Not every teacher checks email often. Some check only in school because they like to leave most of their job in the building.

I tend to answer more after or before school hours because that's when I have the time. I also answer emails on weekends.

I'm not saying parents should never contact a teacher about grades.
I'm saying that if your child is old enough to think about driving a car, fill out college applications, go out on dates, and so forth, they're also old enough to initiate contact about grade concerns.

High school students should be capable of making their own appointments for extra help and taking a missed test. If a student gets a low score and wants to know why, they should arrange to meet the teacher to go over the assessment.

If the student has reached out, and there's still a problem, then step in. But let them try first. School should be a safe place to learn skills. Raising genuine concerns with somebody should be learned at some point.

If you want a compromise, have the student with you as you initiate contact, then have the student write the next email with you there as support. (I'm aware this takes a special kind of relationship between you and the student in your care.)

Find the method that works for your child. The contact could also be in person.
Generally, conversations about makeups go like this:

Student: When can I make up the test?

Teacher: I have these times free ... you tell me what works for you.

Takeaways:
- Judging when to let your child initiate contact with teachers can be difficult.
- It's nice to do things for your child, but building strong communications skills is also important.

Chapter 26:
Student Profile: The Chronic Assessment-Avoider

Introduction:

Dear Reader,

I'm not sure which grade starts the test avoidance thing. My guess is sometime in middle school, when regular tests and quizzes become higher stakes. We can talk about testing as an idea later, but for now, let's just go with the assumption that the assessments are mostly tests or quizzes.

I'm calling it assessment-avoidance because that's a little broader, covering tests, quizzes, projects, and presentations.

In a slight break from normal procedures, I'd like to address this to parents and teachers. Many Chapters have a distinct audience of one or the other.

~Ann

Who is the Chronic Assessment-Avoider?

This is the student who does not take major assessments on the day they are given or due for the rest of the class.

Why would someone avoid assessments?
There are various reasons, some better than others, of course.

- Test anxiety – The idea of a written assessment brings up intense feelings of failure that prevent the student from doing well, making it a self-fulfilling prophecy. (That's probably an over-simplistic definition.)
- Chronic illness – Some students miss a lot of school in general. That's not really preventable.
- They think the extra time will let them do better on the assessment.

This third type of person is about the only one that teachers can address directly. Parents might be able to reach the first type of person, but it's possible the student needs a professional mental health expert to weigh in.

Does the extra time help?
I'm sure it does in some cases. However, in my experience, students who make tests up typically do worse than they would have if they took the assessment on time.

With any assessment, one can usually predict how students are going to do based on past performances. Strong students tend to do well, and weaker students struggle. But even strong students tend not to score as high as they might have if taking the test on time.

Possible reasons for this grade drop:
- The student will miss the questions raised by other students. Teachers may or may not answer questions directly, depending on the quality, but if there's a common misconception, the teacher might provide more direction during the regular class period.

- Teachers might give additional help or hints in response to earlier classes. Such guiding information may or may not be mentioned when a makeup is done the following week.
- Students have a lot of classes. I don't envy them that. If they missed work in one class, they likely also missed work in a few other classes. Handling multiple makeups can be stressful.
- Lessons don't stop. Odds are good that more information has been covered.

What can parents do?

I guess this depends on the nature of the relationship you have with your child. You should be aware of how often they're missing school and for what reason.

The world is at a point that it's probably best not to push them to attend school if they're not feeling well, but if there's a distinguishable pattern to just feeling a bit under the weather, at least have a conversation with them.

These days, you have access to teacher emails. If you'd like to investigate a bit and don't expect straight answers from your kid, you could always ask the teachers if there was a test certain days. **Please note:** The straightforward approach with your child is probably best because it shows you trust them.

What can teachers do?

The students who avoid tests become obvious during the first month of school. You could try having a conversation with them. It may not do much, but you never know what sticks later.

- Offer extensions: I let students know they can ask for an extension on assessments if they have a lot on their minds, but I also try to make clear that this is a choice that may or may not help them in the long run. Typically, around the time of the school play, there are a few kids who have worked really long hours for the last few weeks. That's what the extensions are for.

- Remind students they need to make appointments to make up work: This works better with the more responsible students. The less responsible students leave things until the end of the marking period.
- Remind students that makeups are naturally more difficult than taking something on time.
- Contact parents: I don't contact about the absences, but it's an option. I do contact about the missing work on occasion.

Takeaways:
- Some students avoid tests.
- It's not a great idea, but it happens anyway.
- Some will learn it's not a good idea, and some will not.

Chapter 27:
General Opinion: On Teachers and Students Taking Mental Health Days

Introduction:
Dear Reader,

I'm sure there are multiple terms that apply to a Mental Health Day. Not sure when the term was coined, but it's become more prevalent these days.

Whether you're a teacher, student, parent, or somebody else, taking the occasional random day off can be good for you.

~Ann

What is a Mental Health Day?
It's a day off to get away from the job for a moment. It's not a sick day, though there are times that it's very needed, it could function as one.

If possible, I'd file it under a personal day, but if necessary, I also believe it still works as a sick day. (Sick of school/work still counts, right?)

Please note that it's a Mental Health <u>Day</u>, not week or month.

The general purpose is to take a break to be able to refocus or get some mental margin.

When should somebody take a Mental Health Day?
Ideally, you'd want to take a Mental Health Day when you still have the capacity to enjoy it. Try not to wait until you're fraying at all ends.

For teachers, the timing is important. Review days or project workdays are the best to take off, but you have to be okay with the idea that the students may or may not be productive.

Possible benefits:
- Rest
- Have fun
- Recharge
- Catch up – on work, play, or fun work
- Do something you normally wouldn't on a typical day

What do I do with my Mental Health Day?
Most of my Mental Health Days are spent writing because the ability to string that many hours of dedicated writing time together is a rarity. I may try to squeeze in a walk and a nap too, depending on the weather. Time and weather permitting, I might make the walk in the direction of a coffee joint and negate the benefits of the walk with a sugary drink.

What should you do with your Mental Health Day?
Try to do something enjoyable that doesn't take a lot out of you.

Random ideas (may or may not be applicable to your situation):
- See a movie in the theaters
- Go to the beach

- Go golfing or play tennis
- Visit an aquarium
- Get coffee and people watch
- See a concert
- Take a walk around your neighborhood
- Grab some ingredients and bake something fun
- Visit a friend
- Hang out with your kids
- Play video games (yeah, some adults play video games)
- Read a short novel in a day
- Curl up with your favorite furry friend
- Work on a puzzle
- Work on a craft
- Listen to audiobooks
- Refuse to check your phone or email for the entire day
- Nap

Note: These are random de-stressors. If you don't like something, skip it. If your idea of a good time is a bathrobe, some TV, and a special drink, go for it.

Some of the options have a cost to them. If that's not in the budget, go with the low cost or free options. Some of people's stress involves money concerns. You don't want to turn the day off into something you'll worry about.

Why is it difficult for teachers to take off?

- Most of us are control freaks – That's not the whole story, but there is some substance to the idea that it takes a lot of work to get a classroom to function a certain way.
- It messes with the classroom groove – Depending on the students, taking a day off can throw off the groove.
- It takes a lot of effort to prepare subplans – So much so that it's often easier to stick it out.

- Not much gets done when the teacher is away – Lesson plans are often carefully planned out for a few weeks in advance.

Why is it difficult for students to take off?

- They will miss out on some lessons and assessments – Making up stuff is difficult.
- They might miss out on an activity – There's usually some sort of practice or meeting, depending on how involved the student is in school activities.
- Students often have to miss school for normal doctor and dentist appointments.

Takeaways:

- The occasional day off is a good thing.
- It takes some work.
- It sometimes comes with a monetary cost, but it doesn't have to. There are free options.

Chapter 28:
Special Guest: Former Student on Favoritism

Introduction:

Dear Readers,

Please join me in welcoming Former Student back with more concerns.

It's always refreshing to get other perspectives.

~Ann

Dear Ann,

One issue I would like to bring up concerns teachers who practice favoritism towards students based on either academic performance or personal preference.

Throughout high school I witnessed one teacher in particular giving favors and special treatment to several students throughout 10th, 11th, and 12th grades.

What kind of favoritism was practiced?

The same students were always given extra help during study time, and even at times given teacher training in order to succeed on tests better. This created a rift between normal students and the students being given extra help, allowing them to get better grades and better opportunities later on.

My response to the first major point:

I'm interjecting here because there's a lot to unpack, and I don't want to lose threads by waiting until the end.

I've never heard of the first kind of favoritism. In my experience, it's hard to get kids to come to extra help.

Side note: There is a difference between extra help and tutoring though. In the past, I believe there have been a few people who expected extra help to be exclusive like tutoring when it's mostly a first-come, first-serve thing.

As to the second point, that is indeed something everybody should be aware of.

What were the effects of favoritism?

- The culture of the entire school shifted based on this, having the favorite students being overall treated better, getting more chances to do things, and being seen as more successful.
- While, thankfully, this did not translate into later opportunities and career chances after high school, it did allow these students to push ahead and put a general downer on everyone else.
- A general attitude of, *These are the good ones, those are the bad ones,* pervaded.
- The biggest damage was to individual student egos. Some students were left behind in favor of others, based on a teacher's view of possible success.

Do you believe there are long-term effects from favoritism?

I would argue that this damages both the favored and unfavored students.

The damage to the ignored students is easy to spot and predict. However, the damage to the favored students is not as visible.

Many of the favored kids went on to quit college and did not do anything with themselves after high school. (Whether or not this connects with the treatment is hard to say, but it is my suspicion that the two are connected).

I believe these students could not live up to the potential forced on to them by an adult expecting the world, and forgetting they were still 17-year-old kids with zero life experience.

The damage done to both sides is incalculable and lasts throughout life.

My response to the effects of favoritism (short and long-term):

You've touched upon something I've heard of as growth vs. fixed mindset. There's a fascinating YouTube video on it featuring Eduardo Briceno.

Basically, growth mindset would praise working hard at something to achieve a goal while fixed would praise innate ability or talent. You must have worked hard on this, not you must be really good at this.

There's a tendency to want to spoon feed students information so they can pass standardized tests, which makes the teacher and school look good. People go to crazy lengths to protect their egos. I'm reminded of the Youth Services Librarian who had an administrator who would suspend low-performing kids before crucial state testing.

Agreed on the damage to favored students being harder to spot. It's not as easy to see damage caused by *killing with kindness*.

Follow up Questions:

- Can parents really afford to place their children's future in the hands of a teacher who has such an obvious bias?
- Can a parent understand that their child may be completely wrecked through this poor preparation for life?

Closing thoughts:

High school students are not *little adults*, they are children trying to become adults and stumbling through a series of exercises designed to help them figure out their futures.

I question the general moral character of a teacher unable to see this.

My response to the follow-up and closing:

Parents have a choice about what school a child goes to, but they don't typically choose a teacher. Many schools only have 1-2 teachers for each subject, so guidance would make the choice based on the class level.

Oddly, I like your definition of high school. It might be the best one I've ever come across. It's not overly flattering, but it's honest. Teachers enter the profession for many reasons. It could be a paycheck, a career stepping-stone, a true calling, or something else entirely. With no way to predict what kind of teacher one gets, the best course is to work the hardest with what you have.

If you see something, say something, but the only person you can fully control is you. Try to educate. Where that fails, protect your peace of mind.

Takeaway:

- Favoritism hurts both those favored and those ignored.

Chapter 29:
General Opinion: The Ways We Annoy Each Other

Introduction:
Dear Reader,

People annoy each other by breathing too hard.

Whenever any group needs to be in the same space for an extended period of time, saying or doing something annoying is inevitable. Some things on the lists are controllable. Others are not.

~Ann

Things administrators do that annoy teachers:
- Endless rah, rah, yay emails. – I'm not saying an administrator should be all doom and gloom, but a little realism and commiseration would be nice. Personally, I don't mind the upbeat emails, but I have colleagues who do mind.
- Endless meaningless meetings.
- Not listening to their concerns about schedules.

- Not supporting them on parent or student issues.
- Fixing systems that are fine in the endless battle to be better than last year.
- Send evil emails in the morning "Come see me after school." – Even if it's about nothing, that's mentally very difficult to deal with.

Things parents do that annoy teachers:

- Contact the teachers to argue about grades.
- Contact the teachers to ask for a grade change based on perceived student effort.

Things teachers do (or don't do) that probably annoy some parents:

- Not communicate well.
- Communicate too much. – I am guessing here, but it can't be fun to receive an email every day that your kid is dropping the ball in a class.

Things that students do that annoy teachers:
Question and comment related:

- Ask off-topic questions. – There's a time for off-topic, but in the middle of a lesson is not it.
- Ask questions already answered, especially if that answer was less than five seconds ago.
- Purposefully disrupt the class because it's funny.
- Ask to use the restroom every single period then just wander the halls.
- Complain endlessly. – The room is too cold, the room is too hot, the workload in the current class is too hard, the workload in other classes is too much, and so forth.
- Argue about grades.
- Argue about phones.
- Argue about food.

- Complain about wearing goggles in a lab class.
- Whine about (insert anything really. It doesn't take much.)
- Ask about grade changes because they're so close to the next grade up.

Action related:
- Tap pencil, foot, fingers, etc.
- Wander the classroom aimlessly, then sharpen pencils the nanosecond the teacher starts talking.
- Eat in class. – Some classrooms allow food, and others do not. Even if you are allowed food, that usually means an unobtrusive snack. This is not the time to whip out the 4-course meal.
- Chew gum like a cow. – It's one thing to have it, even if the rules say you shouldn't and quite another for the entire classroom to be able to tell you have gum.
- Put their sweaty $8 drinks on the desk.
- Leave grass or dirt all over the room from their shoes.
- Constantly get up. – get a tissue, sharpen a pencil, poke a friend
- Touch (hang on) each other. – teenage boys are like puppies but not as cute.
- Climb counters, desks, chairs and any other available surface.
- Throw stuff, either at the garbage or at each other or both.
- Make paper airplanes and chuck them at each other.

Other:
- Always arrive late to class.
- Not listen to the instructions.
- Smell up the room. – This is more of a problem in middle school and after gym classes. Sometimes, the body changes faster than the mindset of thou shalt get thee copious amounts of deodorant and shower way more than you do.

Things that students don't do that annoy teachers:

- Hand things in on time.
- Hand things in. Period.
- Seek extra help when needed.
- Have a charger for their school-issued device.
- Have a pencil, pen, or other writing implement.
- Answer questions even if they know the answers.
- Use class time well. – Endlessly complaining that you don't get something, straight up copying from friends, leaving the class to wander, and then, complaining some more, are all terrible uses of class time.
- Use extra help time well. – It's not the time to do the stuff that should have been done in class.

Things teachers do that annoy students:

- Talk too fast.
- Write too small.
- Have messy handwriting.
- Not give clear instructions.
- Constantly nag about missing work.
- Get annoyed when asked to repeat stuff.
- Constantly remind of one thing or another.

Can anything be done to alleviate these annoying tendencies?

Hard to say. Awareness is a first—and very important—step.

- Messy handwriting can be helped by slowing down.
- Instructions can be refined over time, but if the students refuse to pay attention, the clearest instructions in the world are going to be useless.
- The nagging for assignments might be annoying but it's going to keep happening until the student in question gets it together enough to hand something in.

- Pick your battles carefully. Everybody has a limited amount of patience. If you can deal with the annoyance, do so. If you can't, say something and work through the thing with the source.

- What annoys some people, helps others, so occasionally, there's a conscious choice to leave things alone.

Grading aside: The simple circle works like this: teacher assigns something, student does assignment, teacher assigns a grade for the work. When the circle is broken, the grade goes down. This concerns some parents. They contact the teacher. The teacher then tells the student to hand in the missing work. If the work comes in, order is restored. If not, the reminders are going to keep coming.

Why remind endlessly?
Because fair or not, the teacher is going to get asked what they did to prevent the kid from failing. Most people want to have a solid answer to that question.

Takeaways:
- People do things that annoy each other.
- Awareness is important, but it may not be enough.
- What's annoying to some is helpful to others, so it's likely to keep happening.
- If it lies in your power to fix, do so.
- If it doesn't lie in your power to fix, release the negative emotion as best you can.

Chapter 30:
Administrator Profile:
The Students' Buddy

Introduction:

Dear Reader,

Let's talk about administrators again.

For the record, I would not want their job. Maybe their paycheck, but not their job.

That's a lot of icky report writing, overseeing, nagging, and justifying of one's position. The job description could be a faulty perception on my part.

I totally get not wanting to be the bad guy, but there's at least part of the job that entails distasteful things like discipline and oversight.

~Ann

Sample scenarios that say the administrator is The Students' Buddy:

Scenario 1: Kid gets called to the administrator's office to have a chat about behavior issues and comes back with candy.

Scenario 2: Kid gets summoned to the office. Kid rolls eyes and mutters, "I wonder what Jane* wants now."

*Sample name used, but the point remains that the kids should NOT be comfortable even joking about the administrator's first name.

Scenario 3: Kid ends up in the administrator's office to complain about too much homework or phones.

Scenario 4: Kid complains about a teacher. Administrator is in that teacher's room within the next 4 seconds with a *how-dare-you* attitude.

There are probably other scenarios, but let's discuss these four.

My commentary for Scenario 1: Sweet lectures.

There are many reasons to have a candy bowl:

- Candy is awesome.
- Candy comforts the weepy ones.
- Candy battles the munchies.
- It makes the room a bit more festive.
- It provides a safe focal place if things get uncomfortable.

I'm not disputing any of those points. However, the candy bowl should be movable. Hide it when a kid comes in for discipline. If they get weepy, pull it out as a last resort.

I understand that administrators want to be seen as approachable, but my main concern is that the kids have trouble distinguishing between *approachable* and *pushover*. Once they peg an administrator as a pushover, discipline becomes much harder.

My commentary for Scenario 2: Use of one's first name.

I might be showing my age here (scary thought), but use of a first name when it comes to someone in authority tends to be seen as disrespectful.

Kids can be full of crap. They might just be spouting off to put up a front for their friends.

It could also be a sign they've lost respect for the administrator in question.

My commentary for Scenario 3: Entertaining complaints.

There is a fine line here. You want to safeguard students from abuse, but you do not want to give them the idea that if they whine loud enough, things in the classroom will automatically go their way.

There are many valid reasons a kid should be welcomed into an administrator's office. Workload complaints are not usually one of them.

Time management is a skill that must be learned at some point.

Side note: The Great Phone Debate still rages and it's going to continue to rage as long as teachers care what the students learn or don't learn and as long as administration decides not to have an official stance on the issue.

The kiddos—even mostly normal ones—turn downright feral when parted from their electronic entertainment systems. That said, some also lack the impulse control to stay off the devices during class time that requires focus and attention.

My commentary for Scenario 4: Taking sides.

I do not like the us vs. them mentality that creeps up but behaving like this—at the beck and call of every whiny child—is going to drive a wedge between students and teachers.

The kids should be protected. Nobody is disputing that point.

The point is that there also needs to be correction. The students should be encouraged to raise their concerns with the teachers at least at the high school level. That can be frightening. Few people actually like confrontations, but it's also dealing with things at the source. This is a vital life skill they're going to need anyway. If that's been tried, then hear them out.

Newsflash: There shouldn't be sides here because it isn't us vs. them.

Fire Analogy:
Administrators should be a bit more like fire.

Fire provides warmth, light, protection, and guidance. However, one does not want to be completely surrounded by fire, nor get too close.

It's something to admire, use where appropriate, but also have a healthy respect for. By that, I mean, one's natural tendency should be to stay near but not too near the fire.

Takeaway:
- Administrators should be nice but not everybody's friend.

Chapter 31:
Student Profile: The Composition
of a Good Student

Introduction:

Dear Reader,

I feel like the last few Chapters have been on the heavy side, so let's spend our time thinking about good students.

Sounds like a mythical creature. Do they exist? How can they be spotted?

~Ann

What people think we (teachers) believe makes a good student.

- Quiet.
- Obedient.
- Smart/intelligent.

You're half right.

What makes a good student?
If asked to identify the good students in the classroom, everybody could immediately spout a small list of students per class who fit the profile, but what is the profile?

I'm sure everybody has a different definition, but if you widened the list enough, I'm guessing you'd run across the following traits:
- Obedient – I'm not sure Americans are particularly comfortable with the word. For classrooms to function well, there has to be a willingness to abide by certain rules. I believe the word has errantly come to be synonymous with pushover.
- (Smart) Hard-working – I'm guessing if you asked teachers to list three things they wish from all students, this would be somewhere on that list. It's not about the number of hours somebody spends on something, it's a willingness to do what's required to understand. This could manifest as handing stuff in or asking for help or both.
- Considerate of others – This could be a willingness to help others where appropriate or refraining from interfering with the learning of others.

Side note: It's part of the universal unfairness that some people pick up certain types of information quickly. Some of the "*worst*" students behaviorally are those who instantly get the lessons because they get bored and start acting out.

- Willing to take small risks (answer questions) – Part of learning something new involves a bit of risk. It's not comfortable to risk getting an answer wrong. There's a reluctance to step out and venture answers to questions. This one might just be phrased as "talks to me."
- Curious about the topic (or at least fakes it well) - This one's in the stretch zone, but it does make things infinitely easier if students engage with the topic being covered.

Why doesn't smart/intelligent automatically make the list?

Extremely intelligent people can teach themselves almost anything. They don't need a teacher, just a good book or a training video.

They also tend to react the worst to setbacks.

Going back to what Former Student was talking about with favoritism, those that are naturally more gifted with the type of intellect that schools can measure are used to breezing through things. Consequently, previous instructors may also have reinforced the idea that they're "smart."

The problem kicks in when something challenges them. They're more likely to buckle because the brain automatically makes the shift from *I got it, I'm smart* to *I don't got it, I'm dumb*.

Good students are those who engage with the lesson. They overcome any initial gaps in raw intelligence with hard work and perseverance.

Every class has a personality.

Unfortunately, it can tend to be defined by a few students with big personalities.

You can nearly always rely on 1-4 students who will always try to answer questions posed to the class. There are various techniques you can try to pry more answers from the class, but it's a lot easier when answers are offered—as opposed to dragged out of—by a student.

Are good students favored?

I guess it depends on which definition we're using.

Favored as in preferred.

Yes.

Everybody possesses a limited amount of time, energy, and patience.

The students who cost less of those precious entities are usually liked more. That's natural.

Favored as in treated differently.

Shouldn't be, but maybe.

I'm sure at some point I've said or thought something along the lines of "Well, I'm going to be over here talking to the people who want to do this activity." I've also walked away from students who made it abundantly clear they had no interest in listening to the explanation I was giving.

This too comes back to time, energy, and patience.

Takeaways (What do good students do?):

- They listen to directions. Things like don't throw pencils aren't there to kill all the fun in the world. They exist for the well-being of bystanders.
- They help others. This doesn't mean cheating. It means explaining something they understand to other students at appropriate times.
- They answer questions.

Chapter 32:
Special Guest Sassy Substitute: Likes, Dislikes, and Resting Ticked-Off Face

Introduction:
Dear Ann,

Kids chat all the time about teacher behavior, and some teachers just don't look happy.

You can tell they don't want to be there, and it makes for a tense classroom.

"S/he doesn't like me." I hear that from Junior high kids alllll the time when referring to a teacher. Being liked is their #1 thing even if the student doesn't follow rules.

Some feel they are pigeon holed as "that kid" and the teacher or other students will never see them as anything else.

In high school they don't care quite as much if the teacher likes them. They are learning that it's just that way sometimes.

Why do some people who don't even like kids become teachers?
~ Sassy Substitute

Dear Sassy Substitute,

That is an excellent question. I'm at once fascinated by the thought of knowing what my kids say about me, yet I'm certain it's an ignorance-is-bliss situation.

Short answer:
People become teachers for many reasons and stay teachers for many other reasons.

Some enter the profession with an ulterior motive. For example, the job was meant to be a steppingstone to another career or to pay bills while someone (a wife/husband) trained in a different field.

Others truly dreamed of becoming a teacher since childhood where they sat their Cabbage Patch Kids down and taught 'em a thing or two with purloined worksheets from school.

I fall into the first category. Teaching fit me, and I grew into the career. But I'd never dreamed of it as a kid. In fact, up through high school, I'm pretty sure I mentally said: Nope. Just no.

I asked a few teachers why they entered the profession. The reason I found most intriguing was they had a terrible teacher and wanted to do better for others.

Long answer:
It's probably more complicated than that the teachers *don't like kids*, though it's important to be cognizant of the kid perception being there.

I'm positive the words *I hate kids* have come out of my mouth on multiple occasions. What it translates to is *I'm fed up with kids right now because of (insert reason here)*.

Chapter 3 talked a bit about the behind-the-scenes parts of teaching and why teachers are feeling overwhelmed. It's probably time for a more in-depth look at some of the stressors.

I think most teachers have developed Resting Ticked-Off Face.

Short list of things that could be causing that face:

- Tax season.
- Parent email.
- Health concern.
- Family concern.
- Recent meeting.
- Finance concern.
- Pending meeting.
- Recent phone fight.
- The internet has been unkind.
- Doing a walk-away from grading.
- Thinking about work that needs doing.
- Feeling run down and in need of a nap.
- IEP (Individual Education Plan) meeting.
- Anticipating going into a troublesome class.
- Plotting how to deal with one troublesome kid.
- Mentally composing a response to a parent email.
- Kid in a previous class found the last good nerve and gave it a good yank.

That's a sampling to illustrate a point.

Relatively few of the reasons have anything to do with kids and probably zero to do with the kid who thinks the teacher doesn't like him/her.

It's important to know that kid-perception can be self-centered. I mean that in the most neutral sense of the word.

As Sassy Substitute pointed out, middle schoolers are wired high on likes and dislikes. It's a murky, confusing, chaotic time of trying to find one's place in the world. That's naturally going to put the senses on overdrive.

So, when coupled with a few instances of being called out for minor infractions (being too loud, constantly turning around, playing on the phone, etc.), the student could easily conclude the teacher doesn't like them.

Is it truly different for high school kids? (The issue of needing to feel liked.)

Yes and no. I suspect they've just learned to hide the hurt and uncertainty a bit better than middle school kids.

Side note: Kids don't often understand that constant reminders (nagging) about missing work, obeying rules, and such mean that the teacher cares what happens to them.

I occasionally tell my students they need to be worried when I stop harping on missing work (or other issues) because that's the moment I cease caring what happens to them on that topic. Beyond this point, if you fail, you fail, and I wash my hands of it and you.

I often refer to class as a show.

There's a grain of truth there. Being in front of a class can take a mental, physical, and emotional toll on a person.

There are two types of loud and repeating oneself is annoying.

Kids can't always tell the difference between loud as a necessity of being heard and loud because the teacher is yelling at someone. To be fair, the two can flip in a heartbeat in classes where the ambient noise is higher because repeating something for the fourth time is difficult to do without some irritation entering the voice.

Takeaways:
- There are many reasons teachers might not be happy at work. Sometimes (okay, so a lot of times), it shows up on their faces.
- Teachers should be aware that kids will make assumptions based on actions, words, and even in-actions.

Chapter 33:
Special Guest Interview with Sassy Substitute

Introduction:

Dear Readers,

I hadn't considered doing these entries in an interview style, but this happened because Sassy Substitute was kind enough to answer a bunch of my nosy questions.

As I've said before, I really want to get as many perspectives on the teaching world as possible, so it was delightful to interview a substitute teacher.

~Ann

Tell me about your subbing work. (This is what I meant by nosy.) How much does the district you work in pay per day?
Sassy Sub: $130. They increased it this year due to a shortage of substitute teachers. Plus, this charter school is only four days a week, so it's a long day.

Me: Interesting. A four-day week. I've never heard of such a thing in the academic world. How long is a long day?

Sassy Sub: 7:40-3:49. Two prep periods per teacher.

Me: Oh. My. Goodness. Yup, that's long. I suppose it cuts out a lot of the wasted time like additional commutes, but some days, I'm wiped out before 3:00 p.m., and we're done by then. I can't imagine trying to fit in extra help before or after that.

Do teachers leave you a plan?
Sassy Sub: Most teachers leave plans. High school is all digital, so the kids see it. Junior high is paper, a worksheet usually.

Is being a substitute teacher hard?
Sassy Sub: Yes. I can only sub one or two days a week. It's physically and emotionally exhausting!!!! How do you do it every day?

Me: Being a normal teacher is different than subbing, but we could learn from some of your tips and tricks.

Bunny Trail - some differences between normal teaching and substitute teaching:
- Regular classroom teachers tend to know the kids better, which can be good and bad.
- Good: As the students are more comfortable with someone, they open up more.
- Bad: As the students are more comfortable with someone, they show more of their crazy.
- Classroom management is a different beast depending on the type of relationship one builds with the students. There's usually a sweet period where the kids aren't sure which buttons to press, so they're on their best behavior. Of course, it could easily go the other direction.

- Substitutes have no pressure to get the kids to perform to a certain level. That changes the nature of the relationship.

Which is easier, middle school or high school?

Sassy Sub: High school is easier. More hands off with the schoolwork. They are fun to joke with.

They mostly have their status and established friends, so they tend to be calmer in general.

Me: High schoolers are calmer? Eh, I guess that makes sense. Sometimes, it's like they don't have a pulse.

Sassy Sub: They pretend not to care. Not caring is cool.

Me: That is very wise. Although I know that intellectually, I'll try to take it more to heart. Students are very good at keeping up appearances and projecting images.

Which grade is the worst to sub for?

Sassy Sub: 8th grade is the worst in my opinion. They are SAVAGES to teachers and to each other.

Me: This is why I do not teach middle school. Bless those that do. I do not want your job.

What are your secret weapons?

Sassy Sub: I have several.
- I always bring stickers and every age group is overly excited, even 12th graders. I also tend to act goofy, and the kids like it. They are already stressed and want to laugh.
- If a student won't quit turning around and talking, I say, "Quit flirting!" and they get embarrassed and stop.
- I also try to determine the usual class disruptors as they walk in and stick to them most of class, so they don't take over.

Me: You have excellent instincts.

Sassy Sub: I have some unruly kids at home, so I have some practice.

Side note on calling kids out in mildly embarrassing ways:
It can work, but it can also backfire. One must have stellar instincts about when to use the technique because if directed at the wrong child, they will have a massive meltdown. That's never pretty.

Second side note on sass:
Only use it if this fits your personality. Middle and high school are filled with enough fakes, and many kids get good at spotting when someone is being genuine or putting on airs.

What do you do if the students are going crazy?
Sassy Sub: If they get too unruly, I turn on music.

Me: What do you play?

Sassy Sub: Currently, *Encanto*, but when kids are taking tests, I'll play classical music.

Do you initiate conversations or do the kids just talk to you?
Sassy Sub: The students are just waiting to be talked to. So, I'll usually comment about something they are drawing or other things.

What do you like about subbing?
Sassy Sub: I like teenagers. They're funny and awkward.

Takeaways:
- Stickers, music, and light doses of sass can be secret weapons for connecting with students. This applies to both regular classroom teachers and substitute teachers.

Kids are funny and awkward. Ultimately, they want to be liked, loved, and accepted. The more the adults around them can show, the better off everyone will be.

Chapter 34:
General Opinion: A Dream About Coins and Cash

Introduction:

Dear Reader,

Teachers have all sorts of dreams. I'm not talking goals and aspirations for the moment. I'm talking about a literal went-to-sleep-and-mind-movie-started-playing dream.

There are the standard dreams about showing up to class unprepared or forgot an important article of clothing (like pants) or forgot to study for a big test even though we've had our grown-up cards for more than a decade.

I don't usually get the normal dreams/nightmares. Mine are much more vivid.

They don't always have meanings, but I believe one of the recent ones does have a meaning.

~Ann

The Dream Part 1:

I recently had a dream about finding money under school bleachers. Though I'm not totally sure what it means, I do feel there's some weight and substance to it.

I was looking for loose change under bleachers and ended up finding cash. First, it was some small coins like dimes and nickels. Next, I found bigger bunches of quarters.

After that, I found paper cash in chunks consisting of folded over stacks of various bills. One had a $500 bill. Not completely sure I have ever seen one before my Google search to find out if they exist. Apparently, they have McKinley on them.

Where I found the money wasn't always visible. In fact, often it was buried deep in the spaces hard to reach.

I stuck the coins and bills in my pocket, but then, I had no idea what to do with it.

The Dream Part 2:

The rest of the dream was a complicated walk or drive from place to place. The space being explored was a school campus that consisted of separate buildings.

I was trying to tell a trusted friend about finding the cash (paper money) and coins. An African American man from the Board of Education was also present too. My first instinct was to tell him too, but I decided against telling him.

I eventually did tell my friend. I think I was asking her what I should do. She was like so? What's the big deal? You keep it. Duh.

The Dream Part 3:

In another part of the dream, my friend and I were looking for my car. We found an Indian/Asian woman doing dishes. She had the name of one of my doctors. She knew nothing of the cash but gave us a flyer for cancer research. (**Side note:** We found my car in a small space near the dishwasher. Yeah, dreams are weird.)

Possible meanings and interpretation thoughts:
Background:
- I have dreamt about money before but rarely finding cash.
- I have been praying that God would show me what to say to kids.

Specific details:
- I think the location (bleachers) is important. It's a place that has housed a lot of people in general, especially students, over the years. This year, kids have eaten lunch in the gyms. For much of this school year, this was the only location students could remove their masks.
- I think money is representative of talent and value.

Interesting bunny trail:
According to a random search engine, in the ancient world, a talent was a unit of measurement. It's often associated with money (at least in my head) because of Jesus's parable of the talents.

Details continued:
- The different size and variety of coins and cash means the talents are not equal. Some are big; some are small.
- The hard to get to location (under bleachers) means kids hide their talents.
- The leaving it behind part means they don't see the value in what they have or are, so they abandon it or give up that thing/talent.

Second bunny trail:
I started crying spontaneously after writing the part about leaving the coins and cash behind and after rereading the part, so I am guessing at least that part is confirmed.

Details and interpretation continued:

- I think the Board of Education guy was a stand-in for administration and other authority figures.
- My reluctance to tell him means I instinctively knew he couldn't help. He'd just find a way to take the money and throw it at a dumb program. (I could be severely biased here.)
- Administration makes the entity run, but they are removed from the classroom frontline. They don't see what teachers can see.
- Teachers miss the time, talent/gift a lot too because we often aren't looking for it.
- Parents miss it too because it's abandoned under a bleacher (hidden from them).
- I think the cancer research flyer was a stand-in for the good that can be done if people use their time and talents well.

Closing thoughts and takeaways:

- I've been thinking lately how hard it is to get to know people beyond surface stuff. To be clear, this isn't a pat relationships-make-classroom-management-easier speech. It's deeper.
- Kids—and I'm sure people in general—don't always know the value in their time and talents. Some people need to be shown how to take their talents and turn them into something that adds value to the world.
- Value doesn't have to be huge or visible.

Chapter 35:
Parent Profile:
The Ultimate Fam

Introduction:

Dear Reader,

I originally thought to call this type of parent (or guardian) the my-child-can-do-no-wrong delusional soul, but that sounded harsh. The current title also works, as does blind supporter.

As with any profile, this is highlighting some extreme tendencies to make some points. Nobody is all one thing constantly. One adapts to a situation.

My hope is that parents can read the profile objectively, recognize if they have such tendencies, and make adjustments to their approach/handling of the situation.

I also want to help teachers recognize such parent tendencies and get some practical advice on breaking through the blind-support phase.

~Ann

Who is the Ultimate Fan parent?

This person always (blindly) takes the student's side on any issue and has a ready excuse to explain away undesirable behavior or lack of progress.

What does the Ultimate Fan parent sound like?

- Kid isn't doing work in class? Well, make your lessons more engaging.
- Kid is disruptive? They're just enthusiastic.
- Kid is talkative? Yes, they like to talk.
- Kid is distracted? Be less boring. Redirect and refocus.
- Kid is constantly on their phone? Yes, they are.
- Kid hasn't handed in homework in weeks? Were you clear that it was homework and when it was due?
- Kid wants a higher grade? You should give it to him/her because they worked really hard.
- Kid should come for extra help? They have a life outside of the classroom.
- Kid punched another kid? I'm sure they had a good reason. Why can't you control a classroom?

Note: I'm aware a lot of this will come across as an us (teachers) vs. them (students/parents) thing.

Summary of the problem:

Blind support creates an adversarial atmosphere around the thing in question be it a matter of missing work or a behavior issue. It automatically means the parent/guardian is defensive. A defensive posture is not the best for working together to address the problem.

Blind support ultimately harms the child.

Note the qualifier. Teachers want you to support your kids. I think part of the disconnect here is a difference in definitions of what it means to support the student.

Types of support:
Support can be physical, emotional, or something in between.

Parent perception of support:
Parents sometimes think that 100% backing a kid is support.

The danger is that reinforcing the wrong outcomes normalizes them. You risk giving the student a temporary immunity shield.

If you've played video games, you know immunity shields run out after a set time. An untouchable character might blunder into a dangerous situation then die when the shield fails. The shield always fails ... eventually.

You do not want to shield them all through high school and have them crash and burn in college or their first job because they never learned how to manage their time, avoid distractions, or control their impulse to be disruptive.

Teacher perception of support: (What should parent support look like?)
When teachers wish you'd support the kid more, we mean check in with them about homework, have conversations about inappropriate behavior, talk to them about the right and wrong time to use a phone, and such.

Yet another analogy:
This isn't a spectator sport. You're not on the sidelines cheering for your kid to score a point. You are part of the proverbial soccer game. They're back there tripping over their own feet in some way.

Your job is to steady them. Call for a pass so you can get the ball back to them. It's a give and take. If you let them chase butterflies (an actual possibility in little league soccer matches), they're going to miss the opportunities to score.

Clarification: Asking for support on something isn't an attack on your child. Typically, it's for their good.

Reality:

Nobody wants your kid to fail or continue to be disruptive. Different priorities exist, but there is a lot of common ground.

Blindly supporting a kid in not getting work turned in on time or being disruptive or self-destructive does not help them. It gives them a false perception of what will help them. In the long run, this is not good for them.

Note: I do have a very lenient policy on late work. While it will fix a grade, much of the original intent will have been lost. Teachers don't typically give work for work's sake. It's there to prepare them for something else. Often, that's an assessment of some kind (test, quiz, project).

What should a teacher do when they encounter the Ultimate Fan parent?

- Try to be clear about what you'd like done. If they have a conversation with the student, what are the pertinent points that need to be said?
- Clarify why you want what you are asking for. How would your suggestion help the child?
- Emphasize quick action. If someone puts an action off by more than a day, they tend to forget or lose the sense of urgency.
- Remind them that you are trying to partner with them.
- If you are a parent and can relate, create common ground.

Takeaways:

- The best parent support is much more involved than blindly cheering your kid on through everything they do.
- Teachers want kids to succeed at school, sometimes that means involving parents.

Chapter 36:
Student Profile: The Social Media Star Wanna-Be

Introduction:

Dear Reader,

I feel old admitting that this wasn't a problem when I was a high school student.

The world has changed. Some of it's for the better. Some of it's just weird.

Social media is an odd beast than sprang to life within the last few decades.

It used to just be kids dreaming of starting the next big boy/girl band or making it to the big leagues for mainline sports (professional baseball, basketball, or football). Even hockey and soccer (football to the rest of the world) were always more niche. These days, it's Instagram, TikTok, and YouTube.

People get paid to play video games for live or recorded audiences, do movie reviews, or just show off their face.

The type of student I want to discuss today is obsessed with the idea of making easy money with one of the social media giants.

~Ann

How do you recognize the Social Media Star Wanna-Be?
- Always taking selfies.
- Always recording friends and self.
- Obsesses over the number of followers.
- Spends free time and class time on social media.
- Obsesses over what people think of their looks and clothes.

Note: Some of the above is normal kid behavior and legitimate social concerns. In moderation, it's fine.

The situation and the dream:
We've created a world where a select few can make thousands of dollars a month through their social media accounts. A select few from those elite can make thousands with a particular viral video because they have the right, highly engaged audience.

They can hop on their thousand-dollar smartphone, fire up the camera, set to record, say anything or just take some pictures (if they have the right looks), and watch the money rack up.

That's the dream. It's a nice dream, but like the dream of being a sports star, it's not realistic for many people for multiple reasons.

Reality checks:
- There are millions of people on each of the social media platforms. That means your content must impress the algorithms enough to get to the right people who will interact and share.
- Compared to the number of accounts, there are only a few stars.

- Algorithms change. What you do one week might work, but if too many people are exploiting some loophole, the company may redefine how things are being distributed.
- Companies are fickle. They don't need a reason to shut your account down or limit who gets to see what you post.
- Hackers are out there. People randomly pretend to be you because it's funny or some other reason that fits their twisted logic.
- World events can shape what is popular and what's not.
- People have relatively short-term memories. You might be their favorite today, but who knows what will catch their fancy tomorrow.
- People are creepy and have different definitions on what is okay and what falls under totally unacceptable behavior. Understand that any content you release to the internet has the chance of being exploited in some way.
- Beauty fades and to some extent, it's in the eye of the beholder.
- Most people fall into the ordinary category and don't have the right face or touching story to make it as an influencer.
- Not everybody can afford the kind of phone that can create the right content.
- We don't see the behind-the-scenes. There's work involved to prep attractive videos and plan the right scripts. Even playing video games with a high degree of skill takes a lot of practice.

What's wrong with dreaming big?
On the surface, nothing. But obsessing over anything at the expense of the moment and other priorities is never a healthy habit to develop.

So, why is it a problem?
It feeds into the idea that money and fame are the most important

tools we can use to evaluate our lives. When you make it, I'm sure it feels great, but what happens if you don't make it to star status? The auto-answer our heads will fill in is that something must be wrong with us. That can't be good for one's mental health.

During the great phone discussion, somebody pointed out that social media drama spilled over into the classroom. High school and middle school drama may look and manifest differently today, but at its heart, it's the same old who likes who, who said what, and the endless social climb.

Takeaways:

- Most things in moderation are fine. The same is true for social media.
- Becoming obsessed with something can turn out poorly, if we don't know where to set our limits.
- Shirking schoolwork for the sake of social media is where there's a turn from okay to now, we have a problem.

Chapter 37:
General Opinion: A Chronicle
of the End of Any Marking Period

Introduction:

Dear Reader,

As I sit down to write this, it happens to be the end of a marking period, so this tale is as fresh as it can be.

No matter what deadlines have previously been given, teachers will inevitably receive a few inquiries about handing in late work or doing extra credit.

It gets worse if one updates grades anytime in the last week of the marking period.

~Ann

A recurring phenomenon:

One would think that by marking period three students would be used to a teacher's grading policies.

I have relatively lenient grading policies, so I've probably fed the beast. Still, I know for a fact that I'm not the only teacher dealing with quarter-end requests.

Quick definitions:
Revisions: students are allowed to make corrections to a graded assignment.

Handing in missing work: students are allowed to turn in assignments that were never completed in the first place.

Extra credit: additional assignments given for the express purpose of improving a grade.

I don't do extra credit, but I do allow students to revise and resubmit several kinds of assignments for an improved grade. They can also hand in assignments that weren't done the first time. The disadvantage of this is that it's graded as is without the possibility of revisions.

The possible grade they can earn for any late work isn't 100, but it is generous. This policy is in effect for all nine to ten weeks of a quarter.

You know when most students take advantage of the policy?
Answer: After whatever deadline I've set up for taking late work has just passed. Every. Single. Time.

Tip: This is why my deadline is always before the true one.

Why no extra credit?
My department made it a policy in an attempt to cut back on these kinds of requests and demands.

Many teachers who could have extra credit choose not to because it's extra work for them and there's a general attitude of there's plenty of other work the kid chose not to do in the first place, let's start there.

The request (made in person or via email) includes some form of this question:

What can I do to improve my grade?

Depending on the student's personality and level of agitation, the email or in-person contact may also include veiled (or blatant) accusations of this being the teacher's fault. Things like if grades had been in sooner, the student would have known to make it up.

Internal response: When have I ever given you an assignment and not collected and graded it? If *you* forgot to hand it in, how is that my fault?

Note: There is some validity to the part about last-minute grade updates. Teachers make decisions on what to count in the current marking period and what to kick to a new quarter. Sometimes, that means grades are entered without much time to turn around and fix shoddy work.

Internal response: Do it right the first time.

Reminder: Not every teacher has a policy where late work is accepted for revision. The same goes for extra credit. Such things are privileges, not rights.

I think students forget that generous policies are subject to the teacher's goodwill and personal philosophy. I structure my class so that you have to try very hard if you want to fail.

Tip: Some teachers artificially create their own ends to a marking period, so nothing is truly last minute. I usually don't do this for the first three marking periods, but that's a decent way to handle the situation. It naturally happens during the fourth marking period because there's some time built in for reviewing for the final.

Productive bunny trail: Never email angry (or upset).

I should make that an entirely separate topic as it applies equally to parents, teachers, and students.

If you're asking for either extra credit or the ability to hand in late work or fix work that was already handed in, you're asking for a favor.

It's not a great idea to imply that the teacher's at fault in any way (even if they are partially responsible for whatever reason).

Why?
- It puts the other person on the defensive. Defensive people are less likely to give you what you want on principle.
- You've turned this into a power struggle. You may not like the outcome.
- You're more likely to make mistakes either in saying something you shouldn't or saying something that could be misinterpreted. Communication is hard. It's even harder when you're not thinking clearly.

The story typically has a happy ending.
The student works like crazy and hands in something. Their grade improves. Everybody's happy.

Sometimes, the grade improvement isn't enough to reach the goal the student or their parents had in mind. C's don't magically become B's, nor do B's morph into A's. It's great when it can happen but try not to expect outright alchemy-level miracles.

Takeaways (Morals of the Story):
- Be kind and clear in all communication and hope the teacher is willing to work with you on grade improvements.
- Don't wait until the last minute. (She said to deaf ears.)

Chapter 38:
Teacher Profiles:
The Confusing Soul and the Lifer

Introduction:
Dear Reader,

I like the compare/contrast nature of presenting the Lifer and the Confusing Soul simultaneously. Guess that makes me a bit of a teaching nerd, but we already knew that.

As with any profession, this life isn't for everybody.

My guess is that the Confusing Soul doesn't last long whereas the Lifer sticks it out for their entire working career.

~Ann

Who is the Confusing Soul? (How would one recognize such a teacher?)
The Confusing Soul could be defined many ways. For simplicity, I'm talking about a person who knows the subject inside and out. Despite this deep subject knowledge, the Confusing Soul struggles to convey the information to the students.

Signs:
- This person practically speaks their own language.
- Everybody develops a unique way of wording questions, but interpreting the Confusing Soul's questions requires students and innocent bystanders to make odd leaps of logic to untangle.
- Confusing Soul genuinely dislikes having to change things to reach students at different levels.
- Students may be left to teach themselves the subject matter.

Side note: The last point is debatable. I'm sure some of my students have felt they needed to teach themselves my subject. To them, I may be Confusing Soul. The difference is merely a matter of perspective. Sometimes, students choose the harder road because they are too embarrassed to ask for help.

Confusing Soul either adapts or quits.
Change can be difficult. Of the teacher profiles, I'd say Confusing Soul is more likely to call it quits.

This is okay.
If the fit isn't right, then Confusing Soul is better off finding a job in a different field. There are many careers that are enhanced by having had teaching experience.

Recall the Teen Services Librarian. She still uses the organizational skills and planning techniques she developed while teaching. (For the record, I am not saying she was a Confusing Soul teacher.) People fall into and out of this profession for a wide variety of reasons.

Somebody will always step into the gap.
Every year, I tell my students to find a career they love because they're going to spend a long time at it.

That age-old adage about trash and treasure holds true. There are people who fall on the complete opposite side. I'm going to call them Lifers.

Who is the Lifer?

A cynical side of me says a Lifer could be identified by longevity (the number of years they put in), but I want to believe there's more to a Lifer than sheer time marked on a calendar.

To me, the Lifer is the teacher who loves the tough parts of the job. This type of teacher also loves the challenge of always making things better.

Who can be a Lifer?

Anybody really, but in general, this type of teacher is either single or has a very understanding significant other.

Signs (How do you spot a Lifer?):

- Rarely takes off – given how difficult taking off can be, this isn't the clearest sign
- Has a visible passion for the subject material – The point also applies to other types of teachers.
- Likes working with kids – I'm not saying the Lifer always wears a smile, but more often than not, there is joy in what they do.
- Enjoys most aspects of the job – The Lifer may still join in the discussions on everything the school gets wrong.
- Goes above and beyond in all things – This is the kind of person who stays up late to make up a new review game.
- Wants to reach the students where they're at – This teacher is willing to try different ways of assessing and questioning students.
- Is usually at school beyond contract hours – Many teachers do this as a matter of practicality, so this one isn't definitive either.
- Is constantly messing with lesson plans – Lesson plans are made to be changed, but only the truly dedicated go back

and alter the plans with things like reflections and stuff to improve next year.

- Shows up at sporting events, concerts, and other school functions.

Note: Most of those signs are seen in other types of teachers. I believe it's more a matter of the cumulative effect than any single sign.

Do I consider myself a Lifer?
Not really. I lack that genuine love for tweaking stuff. If it ain't broke, I'm not fixing it. I'm realistic enough to understand that not every student will love the subject as much as I do. As long as they give me decent effort, we're good.

Reception by others:
The Lifer is well-liked by students, parents, and peers. Some peers may not understand the Lifer and look at them oddly, but there's also real respect for their passion.

What's the main difference?
Attitude. Confusing Soul gets frustrated if the students don't understand. The Lifer gets excited by the challenge of reaching students.

What do you do if you get a Confusing Soul teacher?
You might have to work harder. This is going to happen at some point in your life. I guess take it as a miniature life lesson on dealing with people who are difficult to communicate with.

Communication is a two-way thing. Do your best to bridge the gap. There's always some adaptation on the student's part to various teacher quirks. Add it to the list of things to unravel.

Takeaways:
- Confusing Soul could become a Lifer, but there's a tough journey in between.

- School challenges share many similarities. Attitude can make all the difference between failure and success.

Chapter 39:
School Problems: Anxiety – Sassy
Substitute Reports a Success Story

Introduction:
Dear Ann,

I witnessed something amazing today.

During my first three days subbing last November, and a few times since, there was a student I'll call D that was in my classes.

D was always extremely anxious to the point of cowering. He wouldn't communicate much with anyone. He had a few friends, but they were mostly emotional protectors.

Once, when he was off-task and had been reminded a few times to get back on task, he blew up at me. I was told it happens a lot. So, I mostly tried to leave him alone because he couldn't handle much interaction. It looked like he was afraid the world was going to crumble on top of him.

About six months later...
I saw D today. This kid is a million times different. I kept checking

the name to make sure it was the same kid.

Today, he sat upright the entire class period. He even interacted with me and the other students. I didn't see one hint of anxiety. D laughed with his classmates, even prompting some of the laughter.

I couldn't believe it! This kid was barely functional only a few months ago, and now he's thriving. His personality shone through as bright and funny.

I don't know what has changed in this young man's life, but he is a different person from November/December. It's like he had some blockage when I first met him and now whatever it is, it's gone and nothing's in his way. I'm so amazed and happy for him.

~Sassy Substitute

My response:
I love this story. It is so easy to focus on the negative things, but we need to hear more of the good that happens.

I'd love to be a fly on the wall and get a behind-the-scenes look at what changed for the kid.

Maybe a family issue resolved, or his parents and doctor found him a good anti-anxiety medication. Maybe he conquered the mental and emotional issues alone or with some dedicated friends.

Is anxiety on the rise?
The impression I've gotten is that the amount of 504 plans for anxiety related issues is on the rise, but that could just be me being less oblivious to what was always there. Maybe the world is just getting better (or worse?) at defining things like anxiety.

I should talk about 504 and Individualized Education Plans (IEPs) soon.

There are many flavors of anxiety. Everything from general

anxiety to post-traumatic stress to being prone to panic attacks falls under the header of anxiety disorders. (Thanks, Google.)

I have known people with moderate to severe social anxiety. At some point in life, we've all felt the gut-wrenching uncertainty of not knowing what to do or say in a social situation. I can only imagine what that must be like when it's almost every social situation.

What are the signs/symptoms of anxiety?
I think it can manifest differently for people. A quick Google search will bring up more than you probably ever wanted to know about anxiety.

It can manifest as physical or emotional issues. Panic, chest pain, trouble breathing, being twitchy and nervous, and having a distinct, overwhelming sense of dread and doom are all symptoms. Even if one doesn't get every single symptom, you can imagine that doing the school thing is difficult when dealing with anxiety. Stories like this remind me that there is hope for a turnaround.

Life journeys differ.
It's also a reminder that one never knows what every kid, teacher, parent, administrator, or other staff member faces. For this reason, it's good to stand on the side of compassion and empathy.

I like how Sassy Substitute tried to give this kid the space he needed while in her class. She didn't hold it against him when he lashed out at her because she got the forewarning that it happens. Sometimes, action is required. Sometimes, people need space and understanding to grow.

Note: This does not excuse being rude or lashing out in anger. Substitute teaching is a hard job. They certainly do not need more trouble heaped on their plate. However, while we cannot control the actions of others, we get to control our reactions.

Takeaways:
- Teaching has triumphs as well as trials.
- Anxiety doesn't have to ruin your life. (If you struggle with it, get the help you need whether that be official medical, psychological, or the moral support of friends and family.)
- Everybody has struggles.
- Needing help is simply a part of life.
- Just because one person seems to have it together now does not mean they have always had their lives together.

Chapter 40:
School Lingo: 504 Plans
and Individualized Education Plans
(IEPs)

Introduction:
Dear Reader,

Source: I checked out an article from www.understood.org to make sure my facts were straight about IEPs vs. 504 Plans. You should read that if you want the much wordier version split into two cute columns.

What follows will be more of an informal teacher's perspective on 504s and IEPs. I gathered some of the information in an informal interview.

~Ann

General differences between 504 and IEPs.
- Legality/strictness – If you did a close comparison of the two, you'd find a common theme. Individualized Education Plans are stricter (have more governing rules to

abide by) and are more legally binding. 504s are legally binding as well, but there's less guidance on what it absolutely must have in it.

- Obtaining one – To qualify for an IEP, the student must have one of a narrow list of disabilities. 504s get handed out like candy because it can be applied for any disability. (Translation: It is MUCH easier to obtain a 504.) Here, disability can be defined very loosely as something that affects the kid's ability to learn. This covers things like gastrointestinal issues, social anxiety, anxiety, select mutism, and behavioral things like oppositional defiance issues (kid is feisty and combative).

- Recognition by colleges – The law that IEPs are based on does not apply to colleges, so they're not required to provide them. 504s or something with similar supports may exist in college. For example, the institution may provide a notetaker.

- In terms of the students themselves, it's generally easier to pin down why a kid with an IEP has one. There's usually a more distinct, easy to define problem being presented, an actual learning disability.

- An IEP must be a (rather lengthy, long-winded, 15+ page) written document. 504s are often written documents, but they don't technically have to be.

- In both cases, teachers have to sign off on having read, understood, and (implied) agreed to implement the IEP or 504 Plan.

- IEPs are more likely with cognitive issues. There is a disconnect between taking in and processing and producing knowledge. 504s are more likely with physical issues (cancer, diabetes, stomach issues, etc).

Layman's terms of how the plans are unpacked.

In short, an IEP dictates how to teach the child while a 504 Plan governs more about what the student can do.

Please note: I am purposefully not reading any specific IEP or 504 Plan as I write this. These are general things that have cropped up over multiple examples.

What are some common IEP accommodations?

- Preferential seating – Usually, the teacher has to ask for clarification on this. It often means close to the teacher and away from distractions.
- Small group testing.
- Extended times on tests, quizzes, or projects.
- Chunking projects into smaller bits (more due dates for parts of the project).
- Modifications to tests – i.e. Less choices on multiple choice. Fewer math problems. Easier math problems.

What are some common 504 accommodations?

- Unrestricted access to the restroom.
- Access to a private restroom.
- Breaks to walk the halls.
- Permission to have snacks any time. This can be a problem in rooms that aren't supposed to have any food in them (labs), but something can be worked out in private with the student who needs that accommodation.
- Preferential seating.

Two types of IEP kids:

- Let's pretend this doesn't exist. I'll do my best.
- How dare you make me do anything? I have an IEP don't you know?

Important side note: Learning disability doesn't mean dumb. Kids with IEPs have been among the best students I've had. 504 kids are more of a mixed bag of crazy, but that's because of the wider range of things that will result in such a plan.

Attitude can be everything. This holds true from a teaching and a student standpoint.

Does it get ugly?
Sometimes. Schools and parents both want what's ultimately best for the student, but there can be a stark difference of opinion here.

It's hard to maintain a balance. Two opinions:
- Let's smother the kids with support to help them be the best they can be here and now.
- We're trying to prepare kids for their future. Let's let them struggle a little here and now so they can fail in a safe environment. If they can learn from the experience now, they'll be better able to handle future problems.

I've not formally picked a side in that debate, but I can see both having valid points. The true answer is probably something annoying like they're both absolutely correct, but the philosophy that needs to be applied for the best results will vary from student to student.

Closing thoughts:
It's good to have the legal protections in place, but honestly, most of the accommodations like extended time are available to all my students upon proper request. I'm not a mind reader (unfortunately), but if a student requests an extension for a test or a project, I generally grant it.

Takeaways:
- 504s are easier to get than IEPs.
- The things that prevent learning can be long-term or temporary.

- IEPs are more likely with cognitive issues. 504s are more likely with physical issues (cancer, diabetes, etc.).

Both types of plans exist to help students reach their full potential.

Chapter 41:
Special Guest: Frustrated Science Teacher – Multiple Preps

Introduction:

Dear Ann,

In one school, I taught Environmental Science, Physics, and Chemistry in the same year.

A friend of mine was asked to teach Biology, Chemistry, and Physics.

In a different school, yet another friend once had to teach Honors Chemistry, College Prep Chemistry, and Biology.

I've seen many other combinations with both special education and regular ed teachers. Chemistry and Physics is a common one. Chemistry and Biology is another common combination.

(**Side note:** Unfortunately, that one is kicking me right about now.) The problem is that you need to do a mental switch when you go to teach something new. I never felt like I could get good at either or all of the subjects I was teaching.

Something's got to give. The year I taught Environmental Science, I ended up treating it like an elective. I kept my students busy with little projects, regardless of how age-appropriate the activity might be.

About twenty to twenty-five years ago, there was a K-12 Science certification. This meant that science teachers could teach any of the sciences. That helped create this problem. Eventually, they moved to K-12 subject-specific certifications. I believe they even went further and now have subject-specific K-6 and 7-12 certifications, but that's not going to help until administrators learn to let their people specialize.

~Frustrated Science Teacher

My response:

I certainly agree on the mental switch comment from Frustrated Science Teacher. Even teaching different classes of the same subject and level require some alternate approaches. The magnitude of the mental switch increases exponentially when it comes to completely different courses.

Simple truth:

There's only so much mental bandwidth. As the special guest pointed out, eventually, something has to give. If teachers are asked to prepare multiple courses, their limited time and energy will be spread further.

This can lead to increased stress.

If I get to teach a course I've already taught, it's easier to plan, but on a typical working Saturday, I could easily spend three hours per prep on the lesson planning phase of the job.

So, there is a huge difference in the amount of time I spend hammering out lesson plans in a year I have one, two, or three courses to get in order.

What controls the number of classes offered?
- Number of kids ready to take a certain course. This naturally varies year to year.
- Number of kids at a certain level such as honors or college prep or resource.

Some science classes can be taught by anybody with a subject-specific science certification.
I believe Earth Science and Environmental Science studies still exist in some colleges, but I don't think there's a separate certification for either subject in my state. That might vary from state to state.

The clearest example I can think of is Forensic Science. This is the awesome class that covers the application of science to solving crimes.

It's normal to have the class covered by whoever has an opening in their schedule for the subject.

The problem isn't specific to science teachers or even public school teachers.
- Math certification covers the whole gamut of specific classes: Algebra, Calculus, Geometry, Trigonometry, and Advance Placement versions of calc.
- Special Education teachers can be placed in any class. They often get very bizarre schedules like a history, Physics, and Chemistry or Math and Physics.
- Private school teachers may have it worse in terms of the unpredictability of classes.

Why are private school teachers more likely to have unpredictable and widely varied course loads?
Most private schools don't have to hire certified teachers. If they believe you have the ability to teach a subject, you're in. This opens doors for some people, but it also means there can be a

higher turnover rate.

Smaller private schools are likely to ask their teachers to cover different levels of a subject like elementary, middle, and high school, especially if it's a class like computers.

I once heard of a computer teacher having upwards of 8 preps. By preps, I mean distinct classes the person had to prepare lesson plans for and teach throughout the week. Not every class met every day, so there would be less plans to prepare in a week, but still, that's a horrifying number.

What can be done?
I guess the best course of action is to educate administrators—especially those who have never stepped foot in a classroom—on the importance of letting teachers specialize where possible.
It may not be possible, but I've been in situations where it was possible, the administrator just didn't think of the right schedule until the assignments were already set for the year.

Takeaways:
- Less preps are always preferable.
- Sometimes, multiple preps are unavoidable.
- Where possible, administrators should be aware that minimizing preps helps save time, which allows teachers to do their jobs better.

Chapter 42:
General Opinion: Uniquely 4th Quarter Problems Part 1 – Student Failure

Introduction:

Dear Reader,

Spring brings about many things in the Northern Hemisphere: an end to bitter cold, erratic temperature fluctuations, Spring sports, Spring Break, Spring allergies, rain, and students who can sense Summer coming.

Some schools are headed into the last month. My state is a late bloomer, so our switch from the third to the fourth marking period is just happening now.

Thus, teachers have enough data to use a grade calculator to determine projections about where the students will land with their final grades.

Most of the time it's good or even great news, but what if it isn't? Let's focus on student failure. This is a tough one to tackle regardless of your role.

~Ann

Quick overview of how grades work in traditional school settings.

- Teachers assign work like projects or tests.
- Students do work.
- Students turn in work.
- The stuff gets evaluated and assigned a grade.
- The grades get entered into a system that calculates percentages or whole points.

I can do a more thorough analysis of grading systems later. The point here is that if there's a breakdown at certain points in that chain, the student doesn't get credit (or gets reduced credit) for the assignment.

Potential failure vs. permanent failure:

Do you remember that scene in *The Princess Bride* where the wizard is talking about Westley being only *mostly dead* as opposed to *all dead*?

Almost failed a course for the year is sort of like *mostly dead*. There's a chance for students to turn over a new leaf and carve out a passing score if they can improve their performance in the 4th quarter.

In danger of failing the course:

I believe that is the official comment that goes on report cards in the 2nd or 3rd quarters. Students can land in this position for many reasons, but it usually takes consistent poor performance to get here.

Informing someone they are in danger of failing can be a great motivator because teachers can lay out a plan that gets the students there. Occasionally, the wakeup call works.

Bunny trail about motivation:

- Motivation can be internal – the student really wants to do their best because it makes them feel good

- Motivation can be external – the student must earn certain grades to please parents, earn rewards, etc.

Those with solid internal motivation will rarely find themselves in this position, but it can still happen because of an illness, family problems, or one of many other reasons.

Passing not possible:
If a student's performance in the beginning of the year is particularly poor, they may find themselves with no chance of passing.

Note: It should not be out of the blue. There should be some contact via phone or email about things not going well, but calls can be screened and emails can be ignored. There can also be language barriers and other factors that make communicating the message tougher.

Informing parents and students of a mathematical certainty of failure is much harder than begging them to light a motivating fire beneath their kid.

Sample math:
Every school will have their own system, but here's the crash course version. Let's nix the final in our example, just to make the math easy.

If there are only 4 quarters, each is worth 25% of the grade. If a student earns 40% in 3 of the 4 quarters, the math looks like this:
- .40 x 25 = 10
- 10 x 3 = 30
- Let's say a passing score is 65. 65-30 = 35

The last quarter is worth 25 points. So, it's now impossible for the student to pass for the year.

Early notification of failure:
Some teachers may not even do such notifications before they

absolutely must. I don't think most have to do notifications until the year has ended and the report cards are set.

Kids in this situation usually already know and either don't care or work very hard to project an air of *don't care* to hide their true feelings.

Early notification of failure can go one of two ways.
- Everything stays the same. – The kid hasn't done much work thus far and will continue to not hand in anything and put minimal effort into formal assessments (tests, quizzes).
- The student becomes more of a behavioral issue.

Even if a student is borderline active in a class, early notification could destroy all sense of intrinsic motivation. Thus, most teachers either don't do or dread early notifications of mathematical failures for the year.

What can be done after the news is delivered?
- Love and support the student even more than other students. Failure doesn't feel good. Some are better than others at pretending it doesn't bother them.
- Work through attitude issues. Remind the student they have value beyond a grade.
- Give the student a reduced workload in your class to give them the ability to pass elsewhere. I would NOT put that one in writing anywhere.

Takeaways:
- Notifications of almost failing a course can be good motivators and help students get back on the right track.
- In most situations, failing a course takes a lot of bad choices on the students' part. It's not about forgetting one assignment. It's consistent. Letting them fail can be a learning experience.

- Once a student is headed for certain failure for the year, it's hard to keep them externally motivated with grades, but there's still a difference between giving up on them and helping them through their school career.

Chapter 43:
General Opinion: Uniquely 4th Quarter Problems Part 2 - Senioritis

Introduction:

Dear Reader,

I wrote this one before dealing with student failure but decided to present the heavier topic first.

Let's talk about a thing many students catch as the year comes to a close.

I've never worked in a school that goes all year with intermittent smaller breaks, but I'm sure they have similar problems when it comes to the last part of the school term before the students get their promotions to a new grade.

I discussed motivation some in the last Chapter, but the basic definition for this thing is a complete crash of internal student motivation to do anything school related.

While still something that needs to be dealt with, there's a lot more hope for dealing with senioritis than a student either about to fail or who has already failed a course for the year.

~Ann

Senioritis:

If I threw the term into a search engine, I'd probably get a fine definition, but I've seen it enough to give you an adequate picture of the issue.

Senioritis is a state of mind that creeps over some seniors that can result in poor attitudes and precipitous grade drops.

It's not confined to seniors, but they are the most prone to it. Juniors and Sophomores still have people to impress if they want to get into a decent college. Freshmen have a long way to go in their high school careers.

*While these are the American terms for grades 9-12, I'm sure other countries have comparable grades and similar problems as the students sense the end of the year.

Causes of senioritis (and things that could make it worse):

- Being accepted to a college
- Being very close to passing all courses for the year

Symptoms of senioritis:

- Lack of focus - this is not confined to senioritis
- Lack of motivation
- A so-done-with-school attitude

Is there a cure?

There is no surefire cure for senioritis. Fortunately, it is a temporary affliction with a natural end called Summer's arrival. However, there are ways to work with the stricken and mitigate the effects.

Note: Some of these take a lot of foresight and careful planning.

Second note: The kids get antsy when any break looms on the horizon. It's just worse when that break is Summer. These may be good things to consider regardless of student age.

Teacher treatment and handling of senioritis:

- Adjust the year's lessons so the hard-hitting, mentally taxing units come first.
- Educational yet entertaining movies – Some subjects are a lot easier to find movies that work with the subject matter. Something like Forensic Science has many options because it's a fascinating subject with many stories to tell.
- A serious conversation about responsibility – It may not sink in now, but odds are good somebody will remember it at some point in their future. People often need to hear something multiple times before it grips them.
- Field trips – The way our year is laid out, the weather is nicer, so assuming nothing inconvenient like a world-wide pandemic hits, there are a lot of opportunities to get the kids out of the classroom.
- Breaks and other deals – I have had some limited success with being clear that I have a set amount of material that needs to be covered, but if we can accomplish my goals, they can have the last 5-10 minutes to relax, chat, and play on the phone. It turns into pure phone time 90% of the time, but that's fine.
- Wrap-up projects – These are good for any age. I recommend leaving the presentation part open ended. When given a choice to make a mini-film, create a PowerPoint or Slides presentation, create a Children's book, or a traditional poster project, most kids go with the easiest option. Go with the flow.

Parent/guardian treatment and handling of senioritis:

Disclaimer: These are ideas and suggestions only. How you've raised your kid thus far will determine their effectiveness.

- External motivation – Okay, so it's a bribe. I call this the carrot approach. I recommend caution with this one, but in moderation, this-for-that is powerful motivation. Don't get too crazy with expensive gifts (cars, large sums of cash) or unattainable goals (all A's if your kid traditionally pulls low B and high C scores).
- A serious conversation about responsibility – This one has arguably low efficacy, but it's still a solid one to try.
- Take the phone away – This is the stick approach, but in a way, it's also a carrot. It just doesn't seem carrot-y. You'd be surprised how effective this method is. It works blooming miracles in small doses.

Takeaways:
- Senioritis hits mostly Seniors, but the other grades are not completely immune.
- Planning ahead can minimize the need for a straight-up daily battle for classroom control.
- Parents too have a role in teaching students about the responsibilities they bear.
- teachers.

Chapter 44:
Student Profile:
The Class Escape Artist

Introduction:
Dear Reader,

Every teacher can give you the names of students who leave class as often as possible.

These kids wander the halls, hang out in restrooms, and nap in the nurse's office.

It is simple stuff mostly, and usually relatively harmless on the surface. It's also a pattern of behavior that can be detrimental to the student's grade.

~Ann

Who is the Class Escape Artist?
This student will leave class every chance they get.

Certain students leave every class period. It's entirely plausible to be on a prep and see a wandering student, have them in class and have them ask to use the restroom, and then, be on hall duty the next period and see them yet again.

I have a friend who calls them Hall Wanderers. I'm only going with Class Escape Artist because it's a little wider in terms of scope.

There are a few diseases that may lead to frequent restroom breaks. We're not talking about those. This is an allergy to staying in a classroom for the whole period.

Where do the students go? What do they do?
- Nurse's office
- Guidance office
- Wander the halls
- Hang out in the restrooms
- Get a drink/fill their water bottle

Sometimes the errand is a legitimate bathroom or water break. Other times, it's a bathroom break followed by a smoke-a-vape-in-the-restroom break. Still other times, it's a complete lie and they just want to walk the halls.

Vaping has replaced smoking as the go-to form of ingesting bad stuff. It does occasionally make the bathrooms smell nicer, but it's still not a great idea.

Is it really a problem?
Schools and teachers bear a lot of responsibility for the students under their care. This gives both parties a vested interest in what the student is doing and where they're located at all times.

Mostly, it's more of a nuisance problem. But if anything goes wrong, society's first instinct is to blame schools and teachers.

Side note: Leaving constantly also requires some creative story telling (lies), which is never great to encourage.

There are occasions that I let my students take a brief walk if they have accomplished what I need them to in the class period. I would rather they ask me to go for a walk than lie to my face by saying they're using the restroom but are walking the halls instead.

Every teacher has their system for leaving the classroom. Most are informal requests that get granted.

Some have an actual sign-out sheet. You may think that's kind of nuts, but it can be necessary.

What could go wrong?
Nobody plans for a medical emergency. Throughout my relatively short career, I've seen at least three students have seizures. That's one tiny example of why teachers and schools need to know where students are at all times.

Soapbox moment: Like it or not, we live in an extremely litigious society. People want somebody to blame if something goes wrong, and Heaven forbid they accept responsibility for themselves.

I don't mind students needing to get a drink or use the restroom, but it's annoying when they waste time. I've had students enter, wander the classroom, chat with their friends, and the second we begin actual work, they have the sudden urge to use the restroom. Yeah, right.

What's the academic harm?
Every disruption breaks up the learning.

At the risk of sounding like a stodgy old teacher ... when a student leaves, they're missing instructions, the lesson of the day, or practice and reinforcement time.

Every task that takes some mental concentration requires one to settle into the moment. That's why many teachers start with some sort of warmup activity.

The analogy to working out holds truth. One does not immediately start sprinting unless they want to risk pulling something.

If one leaves that environment and then returns, they have to readjust. Some people are faster with settling in than others.

Many students who tend to leave every class period are not the strongest students, so they're not that great at picking up where they left off.

What do schools do to cut down on kids leaving class? (What can be done?)

- Implement a color-coded hall pass system
- Have a sheet for students to sign in and out
- Give detentions for abuse of the system
- Directly address the issue – Some kids will do it anyway, but many will curb the behavior on their own because they're generally good-natured.
- Implement policies like only one kid can leave the room at any time. That one is hard to enforce, but they generally understand better when it's a sweeping school policy, rather than a rule in only one class.
- Encourage parents to address the issue with the students.

Takeaways:

- Leaving class can be academically and morally detrimental.

It's so subtle that it's hard to pin down as a cause of poor grades or a growing ease with lying.

Chapter 45:
General Opinion: Let's Focus On the Good

Introduction:

Dear Reader,

It is devilishly easy to focus on negative things. As previously stated, I do not want this to be one lengthy complain-a-thon. There are issues that deserve to be raised and wrestled with but dwelling solely on troublesome things is not healthy.

There must be good in the teaching profession or people wouldn't do it.

The answers I got when I asked other teachers what they love about their job resonate with the ones I could generate on my own. It's nice to have the confirmation.

I may not comment on every single one of them, but a few deserve additional thoughts.

~Ann

Things teachers love about their job:

- Social – Kids that come back to say hello
- Social – Supporting the shy and quiet students
- Sweet – The sweet things kids say (elementary)
- Triumphant – Having the yearbook dedicated to you
- Triumphant – Invitations to sporting events, school concerts, and plays
- Triumphant – Being asked to write a letter of recommendation (high school)
- Academic – Watching the kids make progress in a lesson or throughout the year
- Social – Making connections with kids (getting hugs – note: this was an elementary teacher)
- Academic – The light of understanding that enters a kid's eyes when they finally grasp the lesson
- Triumphant – Changing a kid's mind about a subject (Going from "I HATE math" to "I love math.")
- Sweet – Working with these beautiful, bright kids (The way this was written, the teacher meant her whole class.)

Notice that most of these reasons center on the students. While letting them know it's all about them isn't great for their egos, it's true. What teachers love most about their jobs can be summed up in two words: the kids.

Academic gains (the ah-ha! moments):

One pillar of the job is conveying information in a way that students can learn. It's a lot of work, but many high points deal with seeing the efforts pay off.

Eyes are very expressive. With a little experience, teachers can see the exact second something clicks for a student. It's very satisfying to witness. It's like the moment in a book or movie where everything suddenly makes sense.

Social gains:
Students grow up a lot throughout a school year and over the Summer.

Some colleagues and I recently discussed how much kids mature from their Freshman (9th) to Sophomore (10th) year and from Sophomore to Junior (11th) year.

If you need more proof pull up your Freshman and Senior year class portraits.

Seeing shy kids open up a little and having former students return to say *hi* is applicable across every grade level.

The hugs thing gets awkward sometime in middle school (grades 6-8).

Sweet moments:
Students say a lot of mean things to each other, but there are also moments when shots of pure, heart-melting adorableness come out of their mouths.

The younger ones are more likely to blurt if they love you as a teacher. That's probably because they have less filters on what comes out. They also only get one primary teacher in elementary school.

Side note: Words are powerful. A teacher's whole day could be made by a compliment from a student. The same is true in reverse. Students should know they're cherished as people, not just numbers.

Triumphant moments:
These can be academic, but they don't have to be. To me, they're often more the other gains students make throughout the year.

Changing a kid's mind on a subject fits under this category. It's very satisfying to see an attitude for a subject shift from indifferent to genuine affection and excitement.

Kids love to be seen while they play sports or do other extra-curricular activities. It's one thing to go on your own and another to be personally invited to an event.

Although it is extra work, there's satisfaction in knowing a student trusts you enough to request a letter of recommendation.

I've known teachers who have had yearbook dedication on their teacher bucket list. It's unofficially a popularity contest even though only a handful of students dictate things like nominations. Forming a strong enough connection to gain such recognition is indeed a triumphant moment to have and hold.

Takeaways:

- The things teachers love most about their jobs revolve around the students.
- While the ah-ha moment is powerful, it ultimately pales in comparison to the genuine connections that can be forged with some students.

Words are powerful. A few kind ones can change somebody's whole day.

Chapter 46:
General Opinion: So Many Ways to Make a Schedule

Introduction:
Dear Reader,

I'm on the hunt for more special guests but until they pull through, guess it's just me.

Was scrolling through social media posts, as one is prone to do when avoiding responsibilities. Came across a discussion about schedules.

We haven't talked about that yet, so let's dive in.

~Ann

So many options.
You'd think that there would only be a few ways to write a schedule. Turns out, there are infinite ways to do so. I will not blither on too long, promise, but I want to get a variety.

That said, there are some I'm not including because they're outright baffling.

Traditional school schedules:

Sample 1 of a normal schedule – When I was in high school, we had something close to a normal schedule, but I guess that's relative to what you're used to. If I remember correctly, we had a ten-minute homeroom, classes started around 8 and ended at 3:05.

Sample 2 of a normal schedule – Homeroom (5 min), nine periods that are 43 minutes long, followed by 36 minutes set for extra help. Total 7:35-3:15.

My response: This is pretty standard, though I do find the built-in extra help intriguing.

Sample 3 of a normal schedule – 7:35 warning bell, periods 1 through 9 are 42 minutes each.

My response: I'm a little confused on periods 5-7 all being lunch. My guess is that kids get assigned one of those lunch periods and have a study hall or something the other two.

Block schedules:

Tend to have longer classes. The upside of this is that it cuts down on *wasted* class time.

A and B Day blocks – Two morning and two afternoon sessions about 77 minutes in length

My response: That is just too much face time with the kids. I get the reasons for traditional blocks, but 77 minutes is a very long time.

Rotating small blocks – No homeroom, periods are about an hour long broken into 3 morning sessions and 3 afternoon sessions; complication – there are 4 morning periods and 4 afternoon periods; there's a four-day A to D day schedule with rotating drops.

My response: Well, that sounds terribly complicated. Pretty sure I'd need my schedule in my face every single period to get used to that.

Creative school schedules:
Varies by the day of the week – Monday and Friday school runs 8:30-2:30 with some period 0 classes starting at 7:40; the rest of the week it runs 8:30-3:00 unless you have a period 0 class.

My response: To be honest, I've never heard of a period 0 class. Also, I have trouble with keeping the days straight, so this one might drive me crazy.

Variations on the four-day week:
I've heard of this mostly in rural or very small districts. It sounds intriguing.

Pros to a four-day school schedule:
- Catchup day for kids who miss stuff.
- Saves on gas for buses and building utilities.
- Helps with sports if there are games taking place far away.
- Allows for tutoring on Friday morning (or whatever day is off).
- Field trips can be run on a day that won't interfere with the rest of school.
- Teachers and students get a built-in day for all those normal appointments.

Cons to a four-day school schedule:
- Makes the workday longer.
- Scheduling can be a nightmare.
- *Childcare can get complicated.
- Most of the curriculums out there are written for a five-day schedule

*Note: Schools aren't free daycare centers, but it's common for them to be treated as such because many families need two incomes to make it.

Sample 1 of a four-day school schedule: 7:47-4:15 Mon-Thurs with no Friday, has all the traditional school holidays and extra time off near Thanksgiving

Sample 2 of a four-day school schedule: Elementary, middle and high school students do different things on different days. Some days, kids are home, some days they're in the classroom with their teacher.

My response: That scheduling looks complicated. I can't imagine having kids that fall into different schedules.

Sample 3 of a four-day school schedule: Monday to Thursday for week 1 and Tues to Friday for week 2

My response: To what end? That sounds like a childcare scheduling nightmare waiting to happen.

And just when you thought changing the weeks is all they could do ...

I heard of one rural district that goes with a five-day schedule in the Fall months, switches to four-day from November to Spring, then returns to a five-day schedule.

My response: I would love to hear the rationale behind that one. It sounds unnecessary, but I'm sure they had a reason that worked well for their district.

Takeaways (What I learned through this little exercise):

- There is no one-size-fits-all schedule.
- Different districts have different schedules that suit their needs.

- Kids and teachers can adjust to anything. It doesn't make every answer the best answer.

Chapter 47:
Special Guest Interview
with a Math Teacher

Introduction:
Dear Reader,

If your brain works like mine, it filled in *with a vampire* instead of Math teacher. Just me? Ah, okay then. Moving on.

Guess this is an ask-and-ye-shall-receive situation. I recently got to have a lovely chat with a math teacher to gain some insights into that mysterious world.

~Ann

How long have you been teaching?
I've been teaching since the Fall of 2001, but before that, I homeschooled my kids.

Even before that, I taught a BASIC class to elementary school age kids when my oldest child was in that age range.

I guess you could say teaching is my third official career because

I also was a computer consultant in state government and ran a homeschool bookstore from my front room before this.

Having homeschooled and taught in a traditional school, can you do a quick comparison of those two experiences?

Homeschool:

When I homeschooled, I would plan out the whole year in a nice, neat planner and think: *There, my job's done. Now it's up to them.* **(Insert hysterical laughter.)**

We never quite followed the plan, and the kids required lots of input from me.

I taught three different levels at the same time.

I loved it, but it was challenging for a single-threaded person.

Were there any pros to homeschooling?

We could sleep in. That was a plus. We all like to sleep in.

Me: That does sound lovely.

How about cons to homeschooling?

Sometimes, it went late because my middle child was incredibly distracted. I'd be coaxing him along on his homework while the rest of the family was watching a movie or playing a game.

Traditional classroom:

In the classroom, I can keep to my schedule a lot more easily, but a lot more challenges crop up, because kids have things going on that I don't know about.

I'd love to ask as much of them as I did from my own kids, but I just can't, especially in the era of COVID complications.

When you entered a traditional school, what were you teaching?
Writing. I wormed my way into math the next year.

Me: Don't think I'd fight that hard to get into math but to each their own. Some people cringe just hearing my job.

Why did you stop teaching creative writing?
I didn't like teaching Creative Writing because I couldn't figure out how to grade creativity. Grading math is pretty straightforward.

Do kids really hate math?
I teach the more advanced math topics, so kids might find it hard, but if they hated it, they wouldn't be there.

What is your current course load?
This year, I teach precalculus, regular calculus, AP Calculus AB, AP Calculus BC, and Discrete Math.

Two of those only have one student, but the prep is the same.

Have you taught other types of math?
In the past, I've taught Pre-Algebra, Algebra 1, Algebra 2, Geometry, Consumer Math, Business Math, and Linear Algebra. The only courses we offer that I haven't taught are Statistics and AP Statistics.

Do you have a favorite math to teach? Please explain.
My favorite is AP Calculus AB.

I like it for two reasons. 1) It's fresh enough for me that I'm still learning new ways to teach it, and 2) I've done it long enough that I know it well.

With AP Calculus BC, I'm still learning the big picture on a lot of topics. (I think the big picture is important to give kids a framework for how it all ties together.)

Which part of the job do you like best?

The best part is watching the light bulbs go on. I love when someone leaves the classroom frustrated, goes home, works to understand, and comes back thrilled to have learned something new.

What's the worst part of teaching?

The worst part is grading tests. I just want them all to get 100s.

Do you have any advice or comments for parents?

- Most of these school subjects will never be used after schooling is over. What's far more important is the approach your kids take to learning. Do they have good work habits? Do they keep at it when the concepts get challenging? Have they faced an obstacle and overcome it? On the other hand, if they didn't succeed at a subject, could they put it behind them and still thrive in another subject?
- (I have said this to some parents.) – Your son/daughter is a warm, funny, compassionate human being, who looks out for new kids and helps keep everyone cheerful. That's FAR more important than mastering Trigonometry.

Do you have any closing comments for us?

I love it when one of my students goes on to become a math teacher, but I also love watching them succeed at life in general.
Me: Those are some beautiful and powerful sentiments.

Recap and Takeaways:

- Math is cool and a fun challenge to teach. (I might have choked a little saying that.)
- School is less about a grade and more about mastering problem-solving skills.

- The character-building side of school is just as important as the academic side.
- One of the most rewarding things about the teaching profession is seeing when kids succeed at life.

Chapter 48:
Special Guest: Tips from a Yearbook Adviser Part 1

Introduction:

Dear Reader,

Many teachers wear different hats throughout the year. I suppose that's true for any profession, but it's especially true in schools. There are always extra-curricular clubs and programs in need of an adviser.

Side note: Did you know that adviser and adviser are both acceptable forms of the word? Adviser is more popular (thanks, Google). I'm only using it because that's what this kind lady chose to use because that's what is standard in the yearbook world. My soul wants to use an "o."

While some clubs come with a stipend, many do not. The decision to pay or not to pay a stipend is left up to each school. That said, even if there is a small sum of money involved, people rarely run clubs for the money. If broken down by hour, the amount would be insultingly low.

Let's talk about the yearbook. These are heavy, expensive tomes filled with pictures, memories, and the unseen blood, sweat, and tears of the dedicated staff members.

~Ann

Is running the yearbook a lot of work?
Yes! I spend more outside-of-class time on yearbook than I do on all my other classes combined. I have five different classes with five preps, and this is still way more work than that.

Is your experience typical?
I'm not alone in this. I've heard the same from many of my fellow advisers.

Is it a class or a club?
That depends.
- Some get paid for the class and get a stipend.
- Some are paid to teach a class with no stipend.
- Some of us get paid a stipend to run yearbook as a club.

If there is a stipend, it usually ends up bringing in less than a dollar an hour for the time required.

Okay, so it's not about the money. Why do people become yearbook advisers?
- Some people do the job because they enjoy it.
- Some people are stuck in a position that no one else wants.
- Some people enjoy the non-monetary rewards that can come with it, like appreciation.

What are important things that factor into the enjoyment part of being the yearbook adviser?
- loves design
- loves photography
- loves writing

- loves the whole yearbook experience
- loves the delicious knowledge that your efforts will continue to be valued many years in the future

Is there anything else you'd like to add to this part of the interview?

I'd like to add a few words to readers who might want to let their own yearbook advisers and staff know that they are appreciated.

Side note from me: She had a lot of great suggestions, so I'm moving a few of them to the next Chapter to allow for full processing. Many of them also double with ways to make the yearbook the best it can be.

How can you show appreciation for the yearbook adviser and staff?

First, ignore errors.

Your yearbook staff has almost always already seen these, but they can't do anything about them.

Would you berate a football player after the game for every time he fumbled the ball or an actor after closing night for every time he didn't get his lines perfect? No? Then don't talk to us about problems with a book that has already been printed.

If you spot a lot of errors, usually that means the adviser has been stuck helping kids finish their pages and had very little time to proofread.

If you really want to help, you can offer your services as a proofreader for next year! But be warned – this time is rarely flexible. It will occur just before submission on each of several deadlines throughout the year.

A quick peek at the multiple deadlines:

- The school picture section goes in early, along with Fall sports and events.

- Early Spring sports and events will be submitted last.
- Late Spring is usually not covered because of the time it takes to print and bind the book.

How can people who are not on the yearbook staff help?
(Second way) One way is to be ready and willing to provide photos and quotes when you are asked.

Yearbook advisers and staff members can't be everywhere at once.

If you know of a photo opportunity coming up, such as a lab dissection, a cooking day, a hands-on activity, or a sports banquet, tell the adviser. Invite a yearbook staff member to be present to take photos.

If no one can make it for one reason or another, consider taking a few pictures yourself.

Yearbooks generally don't write about events unless they have at least one representative photo.

If you see a great *unplanned* photo opportunity in a classroom or at a sporting event, take out your cell phone and snap a few pictures. Capture emotion and action.

Whenever you have a photo that the yearbook staff might want, send them to the adviser within a few days.

Me: I'll second the few days part because otherwise, you'll forget. If you send a photo after that event's deadline, it's too late to use. Include a few words to describe who's in the photo, what's happening, when and where it's taking place, and who took the photo. These details tell the story of the photo.

Also be alert for good quotes. Jot them down along with who said them (this is important!) and pass them along to the adviser.

Takeaways from the yearbook adviser's advice part 1:

- Don't point out yearbook mistakes unless you're auditioning for the role of proofreader.
- Photos are vital. If you see a prime opportunity for a photo, take it and send it along to the adviser ASAP.
- Quotes are in demand as well. Be sure to grab the quote, some context, and the speaker.

Chapter 49:
Special Guest: Tips from a Yearbook Adviser Part 2

Introduction:

Dear Reader,

Today, we (the royal we) welcome back the helpful Yearbook Adviser.

She has a lot more tips and tricks for packing those yearbooks full of memories and supporting the adviser and student staff members.

~Ann

Recap:

For those just jumping in without reading Chapter 48, the yearbook adviser was giving us advice on how to appreciate the staff and adviser. Her first two tips were: don't point out mistakes unless you intend to help prevent them in the future and be on the hunt for great quotes and pictures.

Details make things better.

Third, remember (and convey) the details that are unique to you, your classmates, and this year.

You may not know, but for every photo published, somebody will have to be interviewed to provide the details.

This might be the photographer, but more often, it is a key person in the photo.

If you're being interviewed, remember that the interviewer is looking for details that aren't obvious in the photo, reveal your unique perspective, and are different from the year before.

My two cents: This ultimately makes the picture more real and memorable.

Can you give us an example of what to say and not to say?
Don't say: "The homecoming dance was fun."

Anybody could say that any time, any year. Instead, talk about something specific that surprised you.

What to say sample 1: "Jay did an epic break dance. I didn't know he could move like that! We were all clapping and cheering him on."

What to say sample 2: "Our group came late, because we went to the capitol building to take photos on the marble steps. When we got to the dance, they had just set out more of the little cakes, and I was so glad we didn't miss them. They were one of the best parts of the dance."

Keep in mind that the yearbook staff aims to capture the most memorable parts of any event through the perspective of someone who was present and involved.

Are there dos and don'ts for quotes?
If you are asked to provide a quote, take a few minutes to

remember the moment. Be descriptive but use your own words. Don't be reluctant, and don't be flippant. You are capturing a memory for hundreds of students, keeping it safe for decades.

How can teachers and other adults help?
If you are a teacher, please excuse the frequent interruptions to your class. Feel free to ask us to come back later, or to send the student interviewee to the yearbook room at a better time.

Help us make the connection, so we can make our book as meaningful as possible for the greatest number of readers.

Let's talk about the finances of the thing.
- Fourth, be quick to buy yearbooks and/or ads.
- The yearbook is a business, and businesses must have funding.
- Buy a yearbook early in the year.
- Encourage others to buy theirs.
- Help fund the costs of production early, so the staff doesn't have to spend a lot of time marketing.
- If your yearbook does ads for grads and/or businesses, encourage parents of seniors and businesses you know to get in touch with the yearbook staff early.

There's a time and place for being direct.

Finally, just share your appreciation the simple, sweet way. A few well-chosen words can make a huge difference.

If you're at a loss for how to encourage yearbook advisers and staff, you can always fall back on telling us directly that you appreciate our efforts.

- Find something in the book that you love, then tell a yearbook staff person or adviser what you love about it.
- Help your yearbook staff know that all the extra hours they put in to produce the book in your hands was worth it.
- If you have ideas for next year's book, talk about those too.
- If you're a student, consider being part of the new staff.

Words of encouragement are powerful.

It could be your words that cause a yearbook staff member to come back the next year with fresh ideas.

Your words could also help a discouraged adviser remember what they love about the hard, often thankless job.

Closing comments:
There you have it, folks. While many of the pieces of advice are specific to bolstering yearbook staff, the general notes of appreciation are applicable elsewhere too. Kindness may not cost a lot, but the value can be immeasurable.

Takeaways:
- Details make all the difference. Make the yearbook yours by being specific about what was unique or special in a picture.
- Buy a yearbook early.
- Buy an ad if your yearbook includes those.
- Be kind to those who run the yearbook. Words of encouragement and random praise can make the long hours of labor worth it.
- I'm going to add one. If you have power over the budget, consider upping the stipend for yearbook adviser. That sounds like a whole heap of work.

Chapter 50:
Special Guest Interview
with the Mother of a Pre-K Kid

Introduction:

Dear Reader,

Welcome to this milestone Chapter of the Dear Ann series.

I've had a lot more fun with this project than expected. When I started, I anticipated it being informative and useful, but fun was not one of the adjectives that popped into my mind.

It's fitting that this Chapter focuses on a mother and her child, who is just starting his formal schooling journey.

It's easy to get wrapped up in the problems, miscommunications, and frustrations surrounding the business of making a school tick. So, it's also good to remember the part schools—and their stakeholders—play in supporting, training, and teaching kids.

Recall the Math teacher's words about the subjects being one of the least likely things for kids to remember. What really counts are the life lessons of powering through problems and working (and playing) with peers.

~Ann

Thanks for taking the time to chat with me today. I heard your son recently started Pre-kindergarten.

Is your son attending public or private school? What went into the decision for where to send him?
It's a private Christian preschool that came highly recommended by several of our church families. Two women who attend our church teach there.

This school was our first and only choice for our son.

Why do you say that?
We wanted him to have exposure to Christian teaching and a structured learning environment with the opportunity to expand his social skills.

What was the process of enrollment like?
I called the director to ask her about the registration process. I also asked her if there was a discount for a pastor's children. She explained about a form for lower-income families to complete to qualify for reduced tuition. I submitted the form, and we waited to hear if their board accepted our son to their roster at half price.

May I ask how much you pay to send your son to this preschool?
We pay $285/month because we were blessed to be accepted for half price.

Me: That's great! But part of me is sad that pastors don't make more.

Did you visit the facilities?
We did not go for a tour of the school, although it is encouraged by the administrators

Did you know your son's teacher?
I didn't know my son's teacher prior to his acceptance into her Pre-K class.

How big is the class?
13 kids

Boring questions alert.

How long does the school run in a day and for the year?
He attends Monday, Wednesday, Friday from the beginning of September to mid-May, I believe. The school day runs from 9:30 to 2:30.

What grade does the school go to?
It's just Pre-K. There are several levels of Pre-K classes offered depending on where the child falls in age and academic milestones.
Me: That's interesting. I knew there was such a thing as Pre-K, but I'd never heard of different levels of it. That makes sense.

What was the best, worst, and most emotional part of sending your son to school?
- **Best part:** Knowing he will thrive in a structured classroom, learn new concepts, and make friends in an environment that I could not provide for him here at home.
- **Worst part:** Hmmm ... I think it was a win-win for both of us, so I really can't think of a worst part.
- **Most emotional part:** Watching my son get super excited to go on the first day. I did a photoshoot on our front porch, and then, my husband drove him to school.

Does your son like school?
He LOVES school.

What would you say to a person considering the same school for their child?
We highly recommend his preschool. Every teacher and administrator has been a blessing, and we feel they have their students' best interests at heart.

Me: That's as fine an endorsement as any institution can hope to garner.

What do you think is the most important benefit of Pre-K?
Good question. What sticks out for me is giving children the opportunity to socialize and learn basic social skills in a safe, controlled environment while preparing their brains for kindergarten. (Apparently, kindergarten is much more cutthroat today than it was for me once upon a time. From what it seems like, kindergarten is more like 1st grade since that's when I learned to read.)

What's next for your son after preschool?
We are still in the process of deciding what to do with him for next year. He is ridiculously smart academically, but his ability to focus and stay on task is lacking, which he'll need to succeed in kindergarten.

The dilemma (two valid concerns):
- Concern 1: He will get bored with the information if we send him to a 2nd year of Pre-K.
- Concern 2: He will be the kid who always gets reprimanded if we send him to kindergarten next year (on top of being the youngest and most likely smallest in his class.)

If we decide to keep him in Pre-K, he will definitely stay at his current preschool.

If we decide to move him to kindergarten, we would love to send him to a private, Christian kindergarten when he is ready, but the tuition cost is a major factor.

I'm curious. What do private/Christian schools cost these days?
Tuition at the school in question is $4350/year.

Me: *does math* $4350/10 = $435 (Yes, I used a calculator. I got the same answer as in my head, but I needed the confirmation.) The number is a little less scary when broken down over months, but still, that is a hefty additional expense for any family to take on.

Would you consider sending your son to a public school?
Eventually, we want to offer him the choice to be a light in the public school, but only if he wants to.

Our desire is to have the first several school years in a Christian school to get solid Biblical exposure and start developing a Biblical worldview with a firm foundation in truth. (Yes, this starts here at home as well, but it should be continued in his foundational school environment.)

Takeaways:
- Many kids love elementary school.
- Private schools are great, but they come with a cost.
- Socialization benefits are high points of traditional school settings.
- It's tricky to know when to keep a child in preschool or embark upon the kindergarten path.

Chapter 51:
General Opinion: Grading Systems –
Total Points vs. Percentages

Introduction:

Dear Reader,

Every teacher has a philosophy that's built on their training, experience, and personality. I won't go too far down that rabbit hole today because I want to specifically talk about grading systems.

Before delving into that though, I'll admit to sharing at least part of the teaching philosophy of the Math teacher interviewed in Chapter 47.

You'll recall that she has told parents that being a warm, caring person is way more important than mastering Trigonometry.

(I'd say there are about 80,000 things more important than mastering Trigonometry, but that's just my anti-Math bias coming through.)

I'm kidding. Mostly.

The point holds true for much of the education system. School is immensely important, but it still needs to be a part of somebody's life, not the entirety of it.

Whether a teacher, student, or parent, one should remember that there's a fine line between dedication and obsession. Dedication is great. Obsession can reach an unhealthy point.

~Ann

Background and general notes:
Education (of which school is the main vehicle for many people) is an important aspect of life.

From time to time, kids do really ask: when am I ever going to use this (whatever the subject may be)?

The best answer I can give them is that direct use will depend on their life decisions. Beyond that, they're learning a skill and a life lesson. The life lesson may be some variant on how to overcome hard things.

Summary of my personal philosophy about grades:
School is only one part of life. Grades are only one factor of school, and in the grand scheme of life, students are more than their grades.

Two grading systems:
- Total Points
- Percentages

Note: Teachers may have a choice as to which grading system is implemented in their classrooms, but there's no guarantee of that.

Total Points:
Every assignment point has the same weight.
Teachers distinguish how important something is by giving it a higher or lower number of points.

For example, Homework assignments might be 5 points or 10 points. Projects might be 15-30 points. Quizzes might be 10-25 points, and Tests might be 30-50 points.

Pro:
Students who work hard but struggle with formal assessments (tests and quizzes) can do decently in the course by consistently doing the rest of the work.

Con:
Students who can't hand in work for their lives are pretty much doomed.

Percentages:
I believe this system is far more common.

Points are used within each category, but the various categories have a different weight. Formal assessments (tests and quizzes and projects) typically have the heavier weight, while informal assessments (homework and classwork) usually aren't weighted as heavily. Projects might be split off from tests and quizzes. Participation might be its own category.

Pro:
If a student tests well, he or she can usually get away with not handing in a few of the assignments that are weighted less.

Con:
Students who don't test well will struggle to score high because that tends to be weighted heavily.

Which is better?
Most students do fine under either system as long as they put in their best effort.

Slackers are going to struggle under both systems, just in different ways.

Note: I'm sure there are more grading systems, especially at different school levels, but I'm sticking to these because they're the ones I've worked with that are more common at the high school level.

Analysis of the two systems:
Total Points gives the students a bit more control over their fates, but if they are lazy early, it can be very difficult to dig themselves out of the hole they prepared.

Percentages (Categories) tends to place more emphasis on traditional formal assessments.

Ultimately, the decision may rest on what kind of class we're talking about. Total Points is great for classes with a lot of projects or participation (like physical education), but the categories can be adjusted as well.

Projects would have a greater weight in a course like General Art or Engineering and Design. I'm not really sure tests are a thing in those courses.

Core courses (Math, English, Science) tend to lean toward percentages.

Takeaways:
- Understanding the grading systems is good but people (even teachers) do not always get to control which is chosen.
- Students can excel or dig holes for themselves under either system. Working hard is always the best policy.

Chapter 52:
Special Programs: Student Teacher for a Day and Other Internship Opportunities

Introduction:
Dear Reader,

Schools have some unique opportunities for teens, but in order to implement them well, you often need a coordinator who has a passion for both the programs and the kids.

It's not necessarily about gimmicks.

It's about finding opportunities to get them real experience.

Things like Student Teacher for a Day are interesting ideas, but like anything, execution can make or break it.

~Ann

Student Teacher for a Day:
On the surface, I love the idea. I think there's great potential, but I'm not sure a day is enough.

It became a fun day for seniors to hang out with some of their favorite teachers, but I'm not sure if there was any benefit to the classrooms with student teachers, the seniors who volunteered, or the host teachers.

Things that should happen to make such a program meaningful:
- Get the teachers on board. – I believe we were sent a random email that said something like, hey, want a senior as a student teacher for the day? Sign up here. That's fine, but there was nothing about the scope or expectations.
- Make it as authentic as possible (part 1). – As is, the teachers planned an activity for the student teachers to run. That's completely unrealistic. I get that students won't know how to submit a lesson plan, but if you want to give them a chance to understand the job, teaching them the basic skill (even with a template) is important. If the student doesn't understand the material to be covered, they'll need to learn it before teaching it.
- Make it as authentic as possible (part 2). – Have the students shadow the teacher for real, not just pop into and out of classes. If the teacher has hall duty, the kid should too. If the student teacher needs to use the restroom, have them grab somebody from hall duty to cover for them.
- Make sure the students buy in. – Students should abide by whatever dress code the teachers do. When I saw the program in action, some bought in and some did not.
- Have some sort of debrief or program feedback. – A generic survey isn't the best option, but it is an option.

Ideally, you want to find out if the students learned something about the job.

- Open it to more age levels. – There are potential benefits that go beyond pretending to be a teacher for a day.

I think you'd need a minimum of three days to run things well.

- Day 1: Student meets with the teacher they're going to shadow to plan the lesson. If there's time, have them shadow that teacher for real as an observer in a class.
- Day 2: Student teacher runs the lesson under supervision of the regular teacher.
- Day 3: Student meets with teacher to discuss what went right and wrong with the lesson.

Note: These days would not have to be consecutive.

A 3-day plan is more labor-intensive for teachers. There's a bigger time commitment.

Other Internship Opportunities:
Schools often have programs that will allow students to volunteer as interns in jobs they have expressed an interest in.

Possible shadow opportunities to check for:

- Doctor's offices – This doesn't necessarily have to be the student shadowing a doctor, though that is more common.
- Dentist's offices – As with doctor's offices, the student doesn't necessarily have to shadow a dentist. They could be shadowing an office manager or a dental hygienist.
- Elementary schools in the same district – This one is very common.
- Local retail store – What's it like to really run a place like that behind the scenes?

- Police stations – Though there may be legalities involved in each of these opportunities, police stations often have Police Explorers and similar chances for kids to learn about the job. My point is that it's not a stretch to find an in for students to learn the behind-the-scenes stuff to policing.
- Rescue Squads – There are already opportunities for students to learn and take Emergency Medical Technician (or similar) classes, so these kinds of organizations probably already have the infrastructure to take on interns.
- Local restaurants – By the time they're in the middle of high school, students should be able to get working papers. It's not too much of a stretch to find places willing to teach them the other side of the business.

Commentary:

I have never personally run such a program, but I've seen enough to know it takes a dedicated person in both senses of the word.

If truly committed to creating such a program, the school should hire somebody for that role instead of expanding an existing position to cover it.

Having someone committed to asking around and drumming up the best leads for kids to work in a field that interests them is pretty much the bare minimum of qualifications for the job.

Takeaways:
- Regardless of the exact location, the point is that an internship can afford one a prolonged look at a profession.
- Internet searches pale in comparison to real experience.
- Giving kids the chance to see behind the curtain of a job they're interested in can be an enlightening experience.

Chapter 53:
Teacher (and Administrator) Profile: Two Steps from Retirement (or Moving On)

Introduction:

Dear Reader,

Teaching isn't the hardest job out there, but it can be difficult. If you've been on social media (arguably not the best place for information), you've probably seen teachers post amusing memes about the job. Often, they're complaints.

Point of clarification: Complaints are a coping mechanism. Admittedly, not the best coping mechanism, but one nonetheless. Complaining does not mean completely-fed-up-to-the-breaking-point, but it can be a warning sign of things to come.

What if the warning signs are ignored and the teacher (or administrator) decides to move on to a new career?

Even if people move on to other schools or other positions within a school, you can usually tell who has one foot out the door.

~Ann

Note: Everything I say will be geared towards teachers, but there's a similar pattern with administrators, so you can also apply the concepts there.

Disclaimer:
What follows will be general observations. Everybody reacts differently to situations, and everybody's situation will be different. Both will affect how one personally makes a transition. That said, it is quite normal for people to hit a flashpoint, move into full burn mode, or diminish into embers.

Quick definitions for flashpoint, full burn, and embers:
Your brain might have just said: *what the heck is this lady yammering about?*

- Flashpoint – The teacher quits the profession mid-contract. I can discuss that one in greater detail later. This Chapter focuses more on the latter two terms.
- Full burn – This teacher is typically moving on to a new career. They don't care much about the current bridges, so they will set those on fire and watch them burn. It can happen to those moving on to a new career within education, but it's more likely to happen with someone leaving teaching altogether but stuck in a situation where they are finishing the year.
- Embers – This teacher is just marking time until they can retire. Their passion for the subject, the students, and the whole profession has been beaten down over time. They can't wait to retire, but they still want the best benefits package they can get.

Retirement vs. moving on to a new job:
Moving on to a new job:
Those who have accepted another position but are finishing a set amount of their current contract usually have their head and heart in a different place.

They may do their job decently, but they're more likely to slack off.

Whether they go full burn or embers depends on their personality and situation.

What characterizes a person in the full burn stage? (signs and symptoms)
More likely to ...
- Speak their mind (for better or worse)
- Not do lesson plans or show up to certain duties
- Take random days off
- Show a bunch of meaningless movies*
- Mentally and emotionally check out from the school

*One of the jobs in my career involved taking over for somebody who got a supervisor certificate and left mid-year. Those students watched a lot of TV in class. I'm not saying that students given a normal curriculum are likely to retain much, but I did find that particular class a bit behind in terms of content.

Retirement:
Those ready to retire are more likely to exhibit embers tendencies. I hesitate to use the term burnout because it's used in other context. In some cases, there's still a passion for teaching, but the years and circumstances have just doused most of the fire. As this person's energy levels drop, they're more likely to turn inward.

What characterizes a person in the embers stage? (signs and symptoms)
- Takes days off in a regular pattern (like every Friday)

- Puts minimal effort into each aspect of the job
- Withdraws mentally and emotionally from the school community
- More likely to say what's on their minds – This can be both refreshing and amusing, but it can also lead to trouble.

Note: Administrators in this position who are genuinely on the teachers' side are amazing to work for. They're under zero obligation to make the Board of Education happy to protect their own jobs. This frees them to do that job of protecting their people to the utmost because the normal consequence (being let go) doesn't have a hold on them.

Did you notice that there are eerie similarities between the two stages described?

I don't think that's an accident or error. The signs and symptoms are the same. The difference is the attitude. Embers is characterized by more weariness while full burn is tainted by bitterness.

I guess you could say flashpoint is full burn accelerated. It skips over the resentment and goes straight to *heck with this; I'm done.*

Response and situation handling:

I don't think there's much anybody can do on a personal level. By the time you see the signs and symptoms, it's pretty much a done deal. This person is leaving and you're going to have to deal with the fallout if they choose not to make it a graceful exit.

There's plenty to be done on a system wide level, but honestly, that's an overly simplistic thing to say. In truth, what will *fix* some schools would be terrible for other schools. Like students, each district needs to find what works for them in terms of creating an environment that supports their people.

Takeaways:

- Attitude and timing determine whether someone leaving the teaching profession is going to flashpoint, full burn, or be embers.
- There's no quick fix that will change the low morale that exists across many schools.

Chapter 54:
General Opinion: Real Life Lessons Taught in Schools Overview

Introduction:

Dear Reader,

I've been wanting to write this article for a long time. I'm calling this an overview because many of the life lessons could sprout their own discussions later.

Schools strive to teach students many lessons that go beyond the classroom. Because schools are a large portion of a student's life, they will naturally have a role in shaping who the child becomes.

Not every lesson is a positive one. There are unintended lessons that can be picked up.

Though there are probably many ways to define the term *life lessons*, I'm going to go with general tidbits of common sense and wisdom that can be applied to situations beyond schools.

I may not elaborate on everything, especially where the main title is sufficient.

~Ann

Bad life lessons (unintended and dangerous):

Unfortunately, schools don't always teach positive life lessons. There are times when unintended and harmful-in-the-long-run messages are given.

- The squeaky wheel gets oiled. – That's an old-fashioned saying that means complain long and loud enough, and you'll get what you need. Please note that need and want can be two different things. At the very least, your situation will receive a quick ride up the chain of command.
- Other people will pick up the slack. – Group projects are annoying in so many ways. There's usually a slacker or two in the group. Unless the group is purposefully arranged to saddle the slackers with each other, there are times when at least one kid can float by without pulling their weight.

Side note: It's a balancing act. Teachers often want to force people to invest in the project because that's where the learning happens. However, they also need to balance that with the idea that if the slackers are grouped together, there's a solid chance they collectively crash and burn.

Practical life lessons:

These are the most universal (widely applicable) lessons.

- Manners are important. – This one should begin at home, but there are many occasions to practice throughout the school day.
- First impressions are important. – If teachers who don't have a student know that kid's name by the second day of class, it probably means he or she is not making a great first impression. (lasting, yes; good, no)
- How to self-advocate responsibly. – Standing up for yourself is good, but attitude makes a huge difference in

how your request is received.

- Good communication is important. – Solid communications skills are invaluable.
- Writing solid, polite emails to adults (authority figures). – Written communications are going to be a part of your life forever. Being able to present your position in a way that is clear and concise will be helpful.
- Good time management makes life easier. – The amount of time we can waste is frightening. Being able to balance the various aspects of life is very important. This can be taught passively through structure and deadlines.

Hard life lessons (sometimes not learned until later and sometimes never mastered):

These are often learned the hard way, through making mistakes.

- Get better friends. – If your friends are leading you astray (into trouble), maybe find better ones.
- Relationships matter. – There's a fine line between joking among friends and just being mean. You also need to learn when the joke is dead.
- Social media can have consequences.
- Attitudes can determine if you get your way. – Attitudes shape how others perceive you.
- Being responsible is difficult but worthwhile.
- Sometimes there are second chances. Take them.
- We don't hit people, even if they richly deserve it. – In elementary schools, they tend to be a lot more literal about these sorts of lessons, but conflicts between students are not confined to the younger grades.
- Sometimes we do things that aren't fun or entertaining. – Some teachers go through grand emotional contortions to make things entertaining, but life isn't about being entertained 24/7. Some things are the subject equivalent of

chores to do.

Good life lessons:

These are also practical lessons, but they tend to have a positive spin.

- Trust yourself.
- Grades are important but they don't define you. – I didn't relax my attitude about grades until well into college.
- Grace in various situations. – People make mistakes. When something is wrong, there is a good way, a bad way, and several shades of neutral ways to handle the situation. Be kind. Be forgiving.
- Don't hold grudges. – Those weigh more on you than on the other person.
- Hard work will carry you far.

Common sense life lessons (oh look, they revolve around phones ... shocking):

- Wearing an earbud while talking to people is rude.
- Phones are distractions and you have no self-control. – Ignoring people who are talking through subject information is rude.
- Putting a phone in a pocket doesn't qualify as *away*. – If this is the fourth time I've had to ask you to put the phone away, you will forget in the next two minutes, guaranteed.

Takeaways:

- People spend many of their early years in school, so it naturally has a strong impact upon them.
- Some lessons are intended. Some lessons are unintended.

Ultimately, it is up to the student to take their circumstances and embrace the lessons or reject them.

Chapter 55:
General Opinion: When Tragedy Strikes

Introduction:
Dear Reader,

One does not need to look far to come across tragedies.

Let's state the obvious part first. The closer one is to a tragedy, the deeper the effects.

As stated in the previous chapter, people spend a large portion of their lives in school. That time often doubles or triples for teachers. It's inevitable that tragedy will strike everybody at some point.

What do you do when tragedy strikes a particular student or multiple students or the entire school? The response will usually be determined by how many people the event affects.

Disclaimer: These are personal observations only. I am not a grief counselor. If you are dealing with a tragedy in your own life, consider turning to family, friends, and mental health professionals as needed.

~Ann

Definitions of various scales:
- Personal – only affects a limited number of people; deep impact to a few
- School-wide – affects an entire class or the whole school; deep impact to a few; limited impact on most of the school
- Statewide and nationwide – much bigger scale; varied depth of impact

Scales and types of tragedies:
- Personal – medical (cancer; long-term Covid-19; surgery); family or friend loss; divorce; homelessness; loss of a pet; car accidents; other accidents
- School-wide – student, teacher, administrator, or other staff suicide; school shooting
- Statewide and nationwide – 9/11; outbreak of war

Note about homelessness: The word often evokes images of people sleeping on the street, but as far as schools are concerned, it extends to not having a steady place to sleep at night. This includes things like crashing at a friend's house.

Sample tragedies I've heard in the last few days:
- Teacher has cancer
- Friend's baby could die
- Freshman committed suicide

Sample tragedies my friends or students have experienced:
- Divorce
- Broke back
- Car accident
- Loss of a pet
- Loss of a parent

- Sibling with cancer
- Loss of a classmate to cancer
- Pet malfunction accident – tripped over pet and was laid up for a while

Note: The following are general but may be adjusted based on the scale.

Possible responses to tragedies as a teacher:
- Maintain business as usual in class.
- Cancel the lesson. Talk to the class.
- If something affects the whole class, maybe send students and parents a blanket email addressing the situation and your response.
- Give extra leeway with due dates and number and type of assignments due.
- If applicable, pray for the people involved and affected the most.
- Think of small, practical ways to help.
- Let the people involved know you are there to lend support.
- Contact guidance.

Possible responses to tragedies as an administrator:
- Have trained professionals on hand to help those affected the most.
- Address the situation in an email to the whole staff, a particular department, or a few individuals.
- Ignore the situation (not recommended for most situations but a viable option).

Possible responses to tragedies as a parent:
- Personal tragedy in your home – Keep the student's teachers, guidance counselor, and possibly the principal informed. You do NOT have to share details if that's

uncomfortable, but you should be up front about the child's possible needs and absence status.

Side note: Due to legalities and sometimes just poor communications skills, guidance isn't always forthcoming with teachers about student situations. You will have an easier time of getting sympathy and the leeway that comes with it if you are open about some things.

- Schoolwide tragedy – Talk to your child about the event (suicide, school shooting, and such). Let your child process with you or give them some space to process on their own if that's more comfortable for them. Get them professional help if needed.

Second side note: You'll have to use your best judgment about how much to share. There is just enough detail and too much information. Stick to facts as much as possible. Put it in an email if you can.

Possible responses to tragedies as a student:
- Personal tragedy happening in your life – Try to be as open as you can be. You do not have to share details. However, the better you are at articulating what you need (a test extension, a project extension, time to recover, etc.), the easier it will be to get what you need.
- Personal tragedy happening in your friend's life – Be their friend. Sometimes, the best help you can be is to be present. Give your friend a small gift. These are the type that emphasize thought more than monetary value. Tell your friend you are thinking of them.

Somebody mentioned that their school has gotten good at dealing with tragedy. That's a very sad statement, but it is the world we live in.

Takeaways:

- Tragedy can strike at any time. That's a disturbing and sobering thought.
- School is important but not everything. Some situations require you to put friends and family first. Everybody understands this to some degree.
- If you need extra time on something, ask for it. Give enough details to get people to know the depths of what you're dealing with. This will help with getting them to understand why you need what you are asking for.
- You are not alone in tragedy. Many have dealt with it before. Tap into their wisdom as needed.

Chapter 56:
Special Guest: Anime Club Adviser

Introduction:
Dear Reader,

Adviser still looks wrong to me, but I'm going to keep it that because I used it previously.

I've never started a club, though I was adviser to the Environmental Club my first year of teaching. That club was well established, so I didn't have to set it up. My obligations involved showing up for meetings. The handful of students did the rest.

If I ever started a club, it'd probably have something to do with writing, so that's never going to happen because I have more than I can handle getting me quality butt-in-chair writing time, let alone kids.

Still, being a curious soul, I wanted to know the process of setting up and maintaining a club.

I'm sure every school has their own requirements, but I imagine they're similar to the one discussed below.

~Ann

Types of school clubs:
- Subject specific – History, Drama, etc.
- Hobbies – Anime fits here along with Chess Club, Video Games Club, and Book clubs
- Service oriented clubs – Environmental Club fits here along with many other offshoots of formal organizations like the Red Cross
- Career-oriented clubs – this is things like the Future Business Leaders of America
- Some sort of fit in several categories – I'm not sure which category would best fit the Robotics Club. It's educational and STEM career oriented, but it's also a hobby.

Reference: Go here (https://blog.collegevine.com) if you want a more in-depth discussion of these and a whole lot more.

How did you set up the Anime Club?
Anime Club Adviser: After a student found out that I was an anime fan, they approached me with the idea of starting the club and asked if I would be the adviser.

Was there any paperwork involved in the setup? (Who am I kidding, it's a school. There's definitely paperwork involved.)
Anime Club Adviser: The students were required to write something similar to a letter of intent. In addition, they needed a small petition to prove interest.

Random Aside: Have you ever witnessed these petitions being signed? It's really quite fascinating. The students who run it generally corner their friends and say, "Sign." Those who value their lives and friendship generally comply.

How did you recruit kids to join the club?

Anime Club Adviser: We advertised during the school's club fair, word of mouth, and posted flyers up around the school.

What is your favorite part of the Anime Club?

Anime Club Adviser: I love the little community that it built for students who may not feel comfortable socially. Sometimes, they get picked on for liking nerdier things. This club gives them a place to be themselves and meet other students with similar interests.

Additional comment from me: Everybody has people out there. Sometimes, it just takes a little extra push to find them.

What is the easiest, hardest, and best part of running the Anime Club?

Anime Club Adviser:

- The easiest part is getting to know the students and figuring out anime shows they like.
- The hardest part is getting students to come up with new ideas of things to do in club besides sitting and watching anime.
- The best part is learning about new shows and sharing them with the students.

Where would you like the Anime Club to go in the future? Do you have any plans for growth?

Anime Club Adviser: I want Anime Club to venture out into doing character development and drawing.

Would you consider running another club?

Not really. Aside from Anime Club and Esports, I don't think I would want to do anything else.

My response: That sounds like a full plate anyway. Running a club or sport should be fun for the adviser.

I think it'd be fun to do something with puzzles or Legos (or some other building toy). If I had the time and mental bandwidth, I'd consider setting up a club. That's not in the cards for now, so I'll just remain on the prowl for more club advisers to interview.

I've always enjoyed seeing the kids in other settings besides a classroom because you get to see more of their personalities.

Some clubs—especially the more prestigious ones—come with a stipend, but most do not. As discussed during the chat with the yearbook adviser, people who run the club don't make enough money for the time investment for that to be their sole motivation.

Takeaways:
- If considering running a club, you don't have to stretch far for something that looks good, just go with something that makes you happy.
- There will always be work involved in the setup and maintenance of a club, but it's also an investment into students' lives.
- Even if a club is small, it can still be productive and meaningful. These are more likely to generate the fond memories students can have of high school.

Chapter 57:
Special Guest: Esports League Coach

Introduction:
Dear Reader,

One of the nice things about schools is that you can be as involved in extracurricular activities as you want to be.

If you love sports, you can coach. If your school doesn't have an opening, check the surrounding area for job openings.

If you love drama, you could help with the club. That one usually involves the fine and performing arts teachers, but I'm reasonably certain that if you volunteered, they wouldn't turn you away.

If you love video games, you could start a club or establish an Esports League.

You'll notice that the question pattern is identical to the last Chapter. That's because this guest is the same as the last one. Teachers often wear multiple hats.

~Ann

Unique things about Esports League:

- It's relatively new.
- The options for who you can play are much wider. All other sports teams need to meet on a physical field to play their game. Video games can be done anywhere in the world, with some logical restrictions like time zones. There's no travel to away games, just a concerted effort to coordinate time of the match.
- There's a strong reliance on technology. There may not be such a thing as a rain delay, but if the power goes down for any reason (car accident knocks out a pole, squirrel deep-fries self by chewing through a wire, etc.), the game will be delayed or canceled.

Random musing: I went back and forth on whether to use the term coach, but since it's considered a sport, might as well go with the lingo.

How did you set up the Esports League?

Esports League Coach: We discovered that during the pandemic there was an increase in popularity for esports. We decided that starting a team would be a fun way for gamers to express themselves and show school spirit.

Me: I'm assuming this means both the teacher and some students made these observations.

How is Esports League categorized anyway?

Esports League Coach: Esports is considered a Varsity Interscholastic Sport.

My response: That's very interesting. Not sure I would have categorized it as a sport, but it does involve many of the same principles, if not the physical exertion. I guess it's more like bowling or golf, which involve skill and precision more than brute force.

As with anything, in order to get good at a video game, one needs to practice.

What paperwork was involved in setting up Esports League?

Esports League Coach: We had to make up a proposal to present to the principal, athletic director, and the head of the technology department.

Me: I would not have thought of the tech department, but that makes a lot of sense. The team has to be able to have the right equipment and network support in order to connect to other teams across the state and country.

How did you recruit kids?

Esports League Coach: We used posters, word of mouth, and the Club Fair at the school.

Me: So, same method as before. Got it. My guess is "hey, do you want to play video games" wasn't that hard to sell.

What is your favorite part of Esports League?

Esports League Coach: I love seeing the students be able to show their skill and represent their school doing something they love.

What is the easiest, hardest, and best part of running Esports League?

Esports League Coach:

- The easiest part was getting interest in playing the games for the school.
- The hardest part is getting the students to be responsible and set their schedule up correctly for practices and games.
- The best part is live-streaming the games and making highlight reels for the games to put up on the school's YouTube page.

My response: New things require adjustment. For some students, this might be the first time in an organized sport. They could be viewing it as a club instead of a serious commitment.

To be fair, the same mentality haunts some regular sports players as well. I believe a girls lacrosse coach recently mentioned a similar frustration with a player coming and going and skipping as she pleases.

Where would you like Esports League to go from here? Do you have plans for growth?

Esports League Coach: I am hoping that our program can grow and become one of the feature sports of the school.

My response: Esports League is in an odd position. It's run more like a club than a sport in terms of practice location, yet it requires the commitment level of a traditional sport.

Takeaways:
- Technology has opened the way for a new kind of sport.
- Video games can be as casual or competitive as you like. There is a big league for video game sports.
- Gaming may not involve the same level of physical activity as other sports, but it certainly requires a mindset of dedication, practice, and hard work to improve skills.

Chapter 58:
General Opinion: The Power of a Kind Word

Introduction:

Dear Reader,

This Chapter will likely be applicable beyond schools.

The main example I have doesn't come from school, but the concept certainly applies.

Today, I want to discuss the power behind kind words.

I feel like this is something emphasized in elementary school—where you have to hold legitimate lessons on not decking people who annoy you—and then largely forgotten.

Honestly, I completely understand why they don't run kindness programs in high school. The kids do need to hear the message, but the amount of mocking would be intense. Also, most of those overpriced program companies gear their stuff for elementary or middle school anyway.

~Ann

Disclaimer: I'm not a psychologist so any observations I make are general common sense and laymen ones. If you struggle with mental health issues, at least consider professional help.

Soap box moment: Everybody has a unique story and mixture of troubles and triumphs. Still, there are enough similarities in the struggles we face to draw comparisons, learn, and grow together.

Power of Receiving Kind Words:
Compliments don't cost much, but they can mean a lot to the receiver.

There's overlap in some of the meanings, but I'm including them because there's also some unique aspects to certain benefits.
- Boost
- Support
- Validate
- Encourage

Without the power to read minds (or killer observation skills), one cannot know what another person is going through each day.

What teachers see from a student in class is only a fraction of the kid and probably a projection designed to set a particular image at that.

One does not need to have a crappy day to benefit from a kind word.

Outside the comfort zone:
Kind words don't have to be given verbally. They can be sent via email if that's more comfortable. However, sometimes, the effort to speak up is part of the gift.

Mini story:
Today, somebody randomly sent me a private message on one of my social media accounts. Essentially, the message was a short thank you for one of my nonfiction works.

The nonfiction work in question is one of my slowest moving ones on Vella. It has a very low read to like ratio, which is a tad discouraging.

I have this book up through normal publishing channels but haven't exactly had the mental bandwidth to advertise it properly and it's kind of a niche thing, which is common for nonfiction topics.

The point is that even a very short thank you note lifted my spirits concerning this work. I didn't even know I was discouraged about it until the burden eased through the application of kind words.

Power of Giving Kind Words:
Though personal benefit probably shouldn't top the motivations list to send out targeted kind words, it does feel good to lift others up.

The tie-in to teaching:
Teaching, like parenting, can be a thankless job. (That's not a complaint right now, that's a fact. And this isn't a lecture either. These are reminders as much for me as anybody.)

I teach in a high school. It always surprises me when a 504 or IEP (Individualized Education Plan) says something like praise and encourage the kid.

Aside: There's a part of me that hates instructions like that because it feels like being talked down to by the paper. It feels like: *You don't know how to do your job, let me tell you how to do it.*

Despite my feelings about being told to praise somebody, it's good to remember that encouragement, kindness, and compliments are all very powerful.

Pithy statement: Words have power. Use them wisely.
We all know this intellectually, but it's easy to nod, smile, and go about our daily business as usual.

Go beyond safe space:
The education community likes to throw around phrases like safe space, which mostly refers to a place to be oneself without fear of bullying. (Yes, that is an over-simplification because safe spaces aren't the topic for the day.)

I really don't like using either safe space or bullying because both get tossed around like pinballs.

Safe space should be the base goal, not the stretch goal.

School should be a place people want to go because it gives them structure, encouragement, and community.

That's the ideal.

Clarification: School should not be a replacement for home stability, but it's a piece of dust shoved under a carpet fact that not every home life is picture perfect. If there is little to no stability at home for a child, it's nice if a school can help meet some of the emotional needs.

Takeaways:
- Genuine encouragement is sweeter than contrived.
- A little kindness can go a long way with somebody.
- You never truly know what will stick with somebody in the long run.

Chapter 59:
Special Guest: Creative Homeschool Queen Part 1

Introduction:

Dear Reader,

One of the things I love about the internet is the ability to connect with some awesome people.

Part of my mission with this project is sharing many different perspectives on the topic of education.

Everybody has a journey. We can learn much just by absorbing those details.

The next guest wears many hats. (Don't we all?) This Creative Homeschool Queen has an amazing capacity for encouraging people.

~Ann

Hi. Welcome. Thanks for taking the time to speak with me today.

First, tell me about your teaching situation. You homeschool, right? How many kids? What are their ages?

Creative Homeschool Queen: I've homeschooled my kids for four years now. I have two boys, an eight-year-old fourth grader and a five-year-old first grader.

Side Question: What do you do for a living?

Creative Homeschool Queen: Right now, I'm an author, a professional painter, and a singer/songwriter. I also mentor other creatives.

Me: Sounds like a lot, but I bet you're never bored.

Second question: Why homeschool as opposed to a public school or a private school?

Creative Homeschool Queen: I had every intention of traditional schooling for the boys. I really hadn't put much thought into it until we watched a documentary about nontraditional schooling benefits.

Still, I enrolled my four-year-old in preschool at a traditional school.

A full semester into that experience, my son remained unhappy. He didn't fuss going in. No tantrums. He simply did not enjoy the experience.

He would tell me, "Mom, there are too many kids there. I prefer six kids at the max."

With a kid possessing that level of emotional intelligence and genuine raw intelligence, I chose to embark on a different journey. One that suited him, even though it did not suit me.

Me: Wow, that is a very high level of emotional intelligence. It's great that he could express that to you. It's also awesome that you listened to him.

What talking points sold you on homeschool?

Creative Homeschool Queen: There's this study that proved nearly all children are geniuses before the age of five. Every few years, this number decreases. By adulthood, it's 2%.

That means, somehow, many kids are getting their natural genius squished out of them.

Really, homeschooling our boys provided little advantage for us. We were working full-time outside of the home at the time. We could barely afford childcare.

It was tough.

But we knew we could give them what they were asking for. A chance to be themselves. To not get their genius squished out of them.

Now, there are many more benefits.

We organized our lives around this new reality! We can travel without a thought. Any time. We can be spontaneous.

We say *yes* to so many things. But it's still a sacrifice. And it'll be worth it.

Me: I think it's easy to say the word sacrifice and not really know what kinds of changes that entails. I'm glad you followed through.

How do you prepare for homeschool? Do you lesson plan?

Creative Homeschool Queen: This year, I decided to design my own curriculum. It's a work in progress, so we are eclectic as far as curricula are concerned.

We mix it all up! My curriculum incorporates holistic life skills, development of independent and creative thoughts, as well as ownership of self-wellness and self-awareness.

Me: That sounds like a great balance.

What do you think are the best, worst, and most fun parts of homeschooling?
Creative Homeschool Queen:
Best part:
- My kids get to see how I craft my entire life. I can't think of a better gift to give them. My husband and I both work from home, so every day they get face-to-face, hands-on illustrations of two creative, loving adults interacting with their family and with others.

Worst part:
- I work from home! It's really difficult to decide when to share my attention with my kids and when to share my attention with work. I love both. And they are both necessary for me to craft a life I think is extraordinary. So, balance, rhythm, and self-discipline are all necessary.

Most fun part:
- My kids are geniuses. They are kind, funny, elaborate literal geniuses. I learn from them every day. You should hear the sorts of philosophies they create. It would blow your mind. And I get to hang out with them every day!

Me: This is a good stopping point for the day. I have so many more questions, and I have a feeling you have a lot more to tell us about your journey as a homeschooling parent.

Takeaways:
- Kids are geniuses, but many lose that creative drive and passion somewhere along the way.
- "[...] many kids are getting their natural genius squished out of them." – That is horribly sad but true.
- Kids have a lot to teach us.

- One of the hardest parts about homeschooling is finding the right balance of school and work obligations.
- Homeschooling can allow for a wide range of skills to be nurtured.

Chapter 60:
Special Guest: Creative Homeschool Queen Part 2

Introduction:
Dear Reader,

Welcome back. I know I could stuff these interviews into giant Chapters, but I like keeping them on the shorter side.

There's no rush. It's good to take time to process things.

If I've learned anything from teaching in traditional schools, it's the importance of repetition and processing time.

~Ann

How do you handle socialization?
Creative Homeschool Queen: Socializing homeschoolers. I have a feeling that parents overthink this.

We let the kids play. We go to parks, the pool, the library, etc. The boys make friends easily.

We even travel across the country to hang out with friends. But we try not to force it or to stress about it.

Our boys love socializing. My younger son is a bit more reserved, and my elder son makes friends with any human he meets.

The best form of socialization comes from spending time with loving adults like us, our grandparents, aunts, and uncles. This is where they learn how to become their future selves. And how they interact with stable, emotionally-nourishing expressions of love.

Do you ever take cool trips? If so, do they become a part of school or just for fun?

Creative Homeschool Queen: Any cool trips we take are part of school.

We document them and discuss and educate while we have fun. We also teach the kids our crafts. So, they learn the art of writing, editing film, videography, and painting.

They do these things with us as often as possible. Our eight-year-old has even run a video switcher in a live broadcast before!

If we go, they go. If they go, they learn.

Me: That's kind of the way education used to be done. Demonstration. Apprenticeship.

Do you have set school time or just a certain amount of stuff to get done?

Creative Homeschool Queen: We have a year-round, four day a week schedule. It's really, really flexible. But we get about an hour done with each boy every day, not counting outings and projects.

Does your state have any requirements/registrations/ paperwork junk you have to do in order to homeschool?
Creative Homeschool Queen: Every county we've moved to has different rules. As the boys get older, the rules change.

I dislike paperwork, but it's not too bad. Right now, we have a certified teacher review them and their work at the end of the year.

Me: I'm not sure anybody truly likes paperwork, but I see your point.

Side question because I'm a curious soul: Do you move a lot?
Creative Homeschool Queen: I guess you'd have to define *a lot.* We probably do?

I really like moving. I'm a bit of a nomad.

So far, the kids enjoy packing up and moving, whether it's ten minutes away or across the country.

We sort of get into a rhythm of moving. And we make sure the kids process the changes well, and that they understand that we are always a family and that our togetherness never changes, even if the walls do.

So, at about the two-year mark, my boys start getting antsy. "We should move! Don't you feel like moving, Mom?"

Our dream is to have multiple homesteads/creative spaces that we can travel between year-round.

Me: Multiple creative spaces sound like fun. Maybe something like Airbnb would have cabins that could be rented by the month. Your boys sound like they caught your nomad tendencies.

What do your boys do in their free time?
Creative Homeschool Queen: One of our great woes is that the boys' friends don't get as much time to play as they do. And sometimes, their friends are tired after a long day of school. Or have this thing called *homework* that the boys just cannot fathom. Both of our boys love video games, so we schedule play time. They also have gaming YouTube channels, so they enjoy watching other fam-friendly gamers.

They love make-believe play, building things, inventing elaborate games, and playing around with our dogs.

Oh, and they love riding bikes, karate class, making songs together, and hitting up the park and pool.

Me: Shhh, don't tell them everything they do is homework.

What would you say to someone on the fence about homeschooling?

Creative Homeschool Queen: No matter how you choose to educate your kids, remember you have a choice.

Don't go with the default answer. Think about it. What do your kids need? What are they asking for with their little expressions?

Who are they trying to become and how can you move everyone and everything out of the way of that becoming?

Once you know what they need, don't talk yourself out of it. Make it happen. Even if it's hard. Or not what you planned.

Most parents I talk to say something like "I always wished I could homeschool, but I'm not cut out for it."

I definitely was not—am not—cut out for it.

But my kids are, and I'm their only shot at a mom in this lifetime. So ... here we go! Every day. Here we go.

Me: I think those are the right sentiments to end with. Thanks again for taking the time to share your homeschooling adventures with us.

Takeaways:
- Education choice is indeed a big one.
- Every place has different rules about the documentation of homeschooling. Paperwork is usually annoying in any

field.

- Many people think they're not cut out to homeschool their kids, but it's a daily learning process that is doable.
- I think it's very tempting to view school as a dreaded thing, but it doesn't have to be that way.
- Every part of life can be educational. Games and trips and general play are excellent ways to learn.

To Be Continued …

Thank You for Reading:

Dear Reader,

This book would never have happened without the Vella program.

Special thanks to everybody who agreed to do interviews.

Schools have all kinds of stakeholders. Each person has a vested interest in seeing students succeed. It's been interesting to hear from some of the many perspectives out there.

There is much more to come. Stay tuned for Volume 2.

If you'd like to keep up with my work, email **devyaschildren@gmail.com** and/or sign up for my newsletter on my website. (**juliecgilbert.com**)

Sincerely,

Ann Y. Mouse
(Julie C. Gilbert)

Love Science Fiction or Mystery?

Choose your adventure!

Visit: **http://www.juliecgilbert.com/**

For details on getting free books